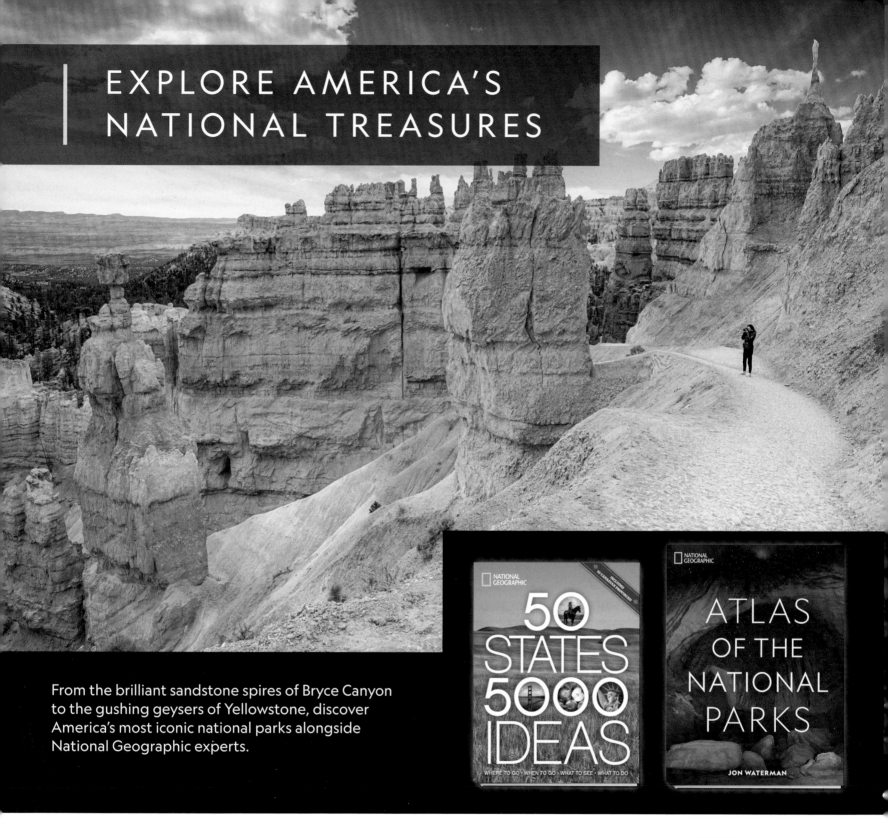

EXPLORE AMERICA'S NATIONAL TREASURES

From the brilliant sandstone spires of Bryce Canyon to the gushing geysers of Yellowstone, discover America's most iconic national parks alongside National Geographic experts.

BOOK YOUR TRIP. BUY A BOOK.

ILLUSTRATIONS CREDITS

Since 1888, the National Geographic Society has funded more than 13,000 research, exploration, and preservation projects around the world. National Geographic Partners distributes a portion of the funds it receives from your purchase to National Geographic Society to support programs including the conservation of animals and their habitats.

National Geographic Partners
1145 17th Street NW
Washington, DC 20036-4688 USA

Get closer to National Geographic explorers and photographers, and connect with our global community. Join us today at nationalgeographic.com/join

For rights or permissions inquiries, please contact National Geographic Books Subsidiary Rights: bookrights@natgeo.com

The National Geographic Image Collection is one of the world's most significant photography archives. Its tens of millions of images capture the planet (and beyond) as explored by scientists, adventurers, writers, and photographers, from the 19th century through today.

The men who founded the National Geographic Society in 1888 did not aspire to create a world-class photo archive; at the time, photography was more the province of pulp publications than scholarly journals. But photographers with interesting images began bringing them to National Geographic.

Some Society board members thought that photos were so lowbrow that in 1906, after the magazine published George Shiras's pioneering shots of wild animals at night, two resigned in disgust. But Society president Alexander Graham Bell and magazine editor Gilbert H. Grosvenor embraced the use of photos, which ever since have been at the core of the magazine's identity and mission.

As early 20th-century explorers and contributors traveled the world, they made images or purchased them from local sources and brought them to *National Geographic*. The photos formed unruly heaps on editors' desks—until 1919 when the Illustrations Library (today's Image Collection) was established. Meticulous librarians cataloged every photograph and artwork, filling them with typed field notes and organizing them geographically: first by continent, then country, then city, and finally by photographer.

The Image Collection's dedication to preserving history through photographs has made it an invaluable resource and an essential reference to vanishing worlds. Governments, curators, and academics often find in our archive the only photographic record of a nation's early history, a lost culture, or an extinct species.

The archive houses important images made by a who's who of photographers: 20th-century luminaries such as Margaret Bourke-White, Mary Ellen Mark, Ansel Adams, and Alfred Eisenstaedt, as well as the leading photographers of today. It's also a visual record of some of humanity's greatest achievements: Amelia Earhart's flights and Jacques Cousteau's dives, Jane Goodall's findings about chimpanzee behavior and Bob Ballard's discovery of the wreck of the *Titanic*. The oldest photographs of the United States are William Henry Jackson's railroad images of the American West, circa 1870. The first color aerial photograph was of the Statue of Liberty, shot from a plane for the September 1930 issue of *National Geographic*.

A vault at National Geographic's headquarters holds 11.5 million physical objects: photographs; transparencies; negatives; albums; glass plates; and autochromes, the first form of color photography. The film collection includes 500,000 films and videos. And the digital collection stores almost 50 million images on servers, with roughly 190,000 added to the archives every year. We estimate we hold as many as 20 million images of the United States in our ever growing Image Collection, including 15,000 of the nation's capital, 200,000 photographs from NASA, and 3,000 images of American presidents.

Every addition to the Image Collection tells a piece of our world's story and furthers Alexander Graham Bell's mission for National Geographic: to illuminate "the world and all that is in it."

FOREWORD BY JILL LEPORE

Jill Lepore is the David Woods Kemper '41 Professor of American History at Harvard University. In 2012 she was named a Harvard College Professor, a recognition of distinction in undergraduate teaching. She has been a staff writer for the *New Yorker* since 2005 and is also the host of the podcast *The Last Archive.* As a wide-ranging and prolific essayist, Lepore writes about American history, law, literature, and politics. She won the Bancroft Prize for her book *The Name of War* and was a Pulitzer Prize finalist in history for *The Story of America,* which was also short-listed for the PEN Literary Award for the Art of the Essay. Her other award-winning books include *Book of Ages, The Secret History of Wonder Woman,* and *These Truths: A History of the United States.* Her book *If Then: How the Simulmatics Corporation Invented the Future* is out this year.

ACKNOWLEDGMENTS

America the Beautiful would not be possible without the time and talent of many at National Geographic Books. A special thank you to creative director Melissa Farris, senior photo editor Meredith Wilcox, senior editorial project manager Allyson Johnson, executive editor Hilary Black, senior editor Susan Hitchcock, senior production manager Judith Klein, and editorial assistant Mariya Khan for their work in conceptualizing and executing this collection. To Erica Green, your masterful sleuthing and persistence filled these pages with the wonderful voices of fascinating people across America— thank you. And to our friends at *National Geographic* magazine and the National Geographic Image Collection, thank you for your support, ideas, and collaboration.

INDIANA A crescent moon hangs in the sky as the sun sets over a shorn hay field. *Derek Dammann, 2013*

OPPOSITE: **MINNESOTA** A woodland caribou bull bellows at a cow and her calf while they graze on the lakeshore in the Northwoods of Minnesota. *Jim Brandenburg, 2005*

PAGE 406: **IOWA** Flags, military patches, and memorial messages decorate a telephone pole that stands along a county road dedicated to United States military veterans. *David Guttenfelder, 2014*

PAGE 407: **WISCONSIN** University of Wisconsin–Madison cheerleaders perform a pyramid with their beloved mascot, Bucky Badger, outside the state capitol in Madison. *Catherine Karnow, 2005*

TOM BROKAW

I am a son of the Great Plains—born in South Dakota, that stretch of mid-continent prairie divided by the Missouri River.

Even though I've been gone for more than half a century, I am still shaped by memories of vast stretches of grassland where bison, elk, and grizzlies once roamed. I keep Sioux artifacts I collected as a boy, and I return once a year to be renewed by the sweep of space and ever-changing weather rolling out of the skies—and I salute friends who have stayed to make the rich soil a vast cornucopia of grain and meat.

South Dakota is where I was born and where I'll be buried.

Tom Brokaw was the anchor and managing editor of NBC Nightly News for 22 years. As a journalist and author, he covered Watergate, the fall of the Berlin Wall, and the 9/11 terrorist attacks. He was born and raised in Webster, South Dakota.

SOUTH DAKOTA Backed by Sheep Mountain, Teton Sioux men ride on horseback in the badlands. *Edward S. Curtis, 1908*

MICHIGAN Patrons dance to Motown hits at Ethel's Cocktail Lounge, a popular Detroit nightclub that once hosted big-time acts, including Muddy Waters, Jimmy Reed, and Little Milton. *James L. Amos, 1979*

MINNESOTA A man lures visitors into the World of Wonders Palace of Illusions at the Minnesota State Fair. The traveling show features 12 acts that include carnival performers and illusionists. *Brian Lehmann, 2012*

ILLINOIS From the "Tilt Room" at the 360 Chicago Observation Deck, tourists hold tight to get a view of downtown Chicago from 1,000 feet (305 m) above the Magnificent Mile. *Stacy Gold, 2014*

MARISSA MAYER

I grew up in Wisconsin and take great pride in being a Wisconsinite. To me, Wisconsin is home to the most incredible people—their work ethic, manners, and warmth are most notable. What I miss most, though, are the seasons—each so vibrant, crisp, and different than the last that it's hard to pick a favorite. I feel so blessed to have been surrounded during my formative years by hardworking people, a respect for arts and culture, and the indelible beauty of Wisconsin's seasons.

Businesswoman and information technology executive Marissa Mayer is the co-founder of Lumi Labs, a startup focused on building consumer applications enabled by artificial intelligence. Formerly, she served as the president and CEO of Yahoo! and held positions at Google. Born and raised in Wisconsin, she currently lives in San Francisco, California.

WISCONSIN A Wisconsin farm plants strips of alfalfa between corn and soybean fields to reduce fertilizer runoff. Fertilizer helps produce plentiful crops, giving plants more nitrogen than naturally occurs in the soil. *Peter Essick, 2013*

OPPOSITE: NEBRASKA Riders swing high in the sky on a ride at the Nebraska State Fair in Lincoln. Nebraska has held a state fair, across multiple host cities, since 1859; it was held in Lincoln from 1901 to 2009 and in Grand Island since 2010. *Joel Sartore, 2007*

PAGE 396: NORTH DAKOTA Children play with a young puppy in the back of a truck in Fort Totten on the Spirit Lake Sioux Indian Reservation. The reservation was established by a treaty in 1867 and is home to more than 7,000 Spirit Lake tribal members. *Rena Effendi, 2014*

PAGE 397: IOWA The Iowa State Fair Queen competes in the annual Llama Limbo Contest. The 11-day fair, one of the largest in the United States, has been held since 1854, and on its current fairgrounds since 1886. *David Guttenfelder, 2016*

IOWA Monarch butterflies *(Danaus plexippus)* flutter onto flowering thistle plants on the prairie. *Jim Brandenburg, 1998*

LEBRON JAMES

Before anyone ever cared where I would play basketball, I was a kid from Northeast Ohio. In Northeast Ohio, nothing is given. Everything is earned. You work for what you have. No matter where I go in the world, Ohio will always be home.

LeBron James is a professional basketball player for the Los Angeles Lakers. He has won three NBA championships and has been named NBA MVP four times. From Akron, Ohio, he was drafted in 2003 by the Cleveland Cavaliers as the first overall draft pick. In 2018, he opened the pioneering I PROMISE School in his hometown, where he works with students and families in the community through his LeBron James Family Foundation.

OHIO A basketball hoop is attached to a fence that surrounds an Amish school in Millersburg. *Eric Kruszewski, 2010*

SOUTH DAKOTA A reproduction of a *T. rex* takes shape at the Black Hills Institute of Geological Research in Hill City. The institute is the largest private fossil firm, excavating more *T. rex* fossils than any other in the world. *Gabriele Galimberti and Juri De Luca, 2019*

MINNESOTA A life-size model of a *Quetzalcoatlus northropi* is painted at Blue Rhino Studio in Minneapolis. For 22 years, the studio has specialized in interpretive design and artistic fabrication of museum, visitors center, and zoological artifacts. *Robert Clark, 2017*

INDIANA Led by the athletic director of Bloomington High School North, the Cougar football team kneels in the end zone to bow their heads in prayer. *Steve Raymer, 2012*

JOEL SARTORE

Why Nebraska? We don't complain, even though the weather gives us reason to. We are honest, since liars don't get much help from their neighbors. We are good stewards, knowing we're all just passing through. Even our state motto is built around doing the right thing: "Equality Under the Law." We protect all among us.

Joel Sartore is an award-winning photographer, speaker, author, conservationist, and the 2018 National Geographic Explorer of the Year. He is the founder of the Photo Ark, a 25-year documentary project to save species and habitat by documenting the nearly 15,000 species living in the world's zoos and wildlife sanctuaries. He lives in Lincoln, Nebraska.

NEBRASKA The Salt Creek tiger beetle *(Cicindela nevadica lincolniana)* is listed as federally endangered, but is in recovery thanks to three protected wild populations, with 500 to 1,000 individuals in each. The beetle is only found in the eastern saline wetlands of Nebraska and is threatened by habitat loss. *Joel Sartore, 2007*

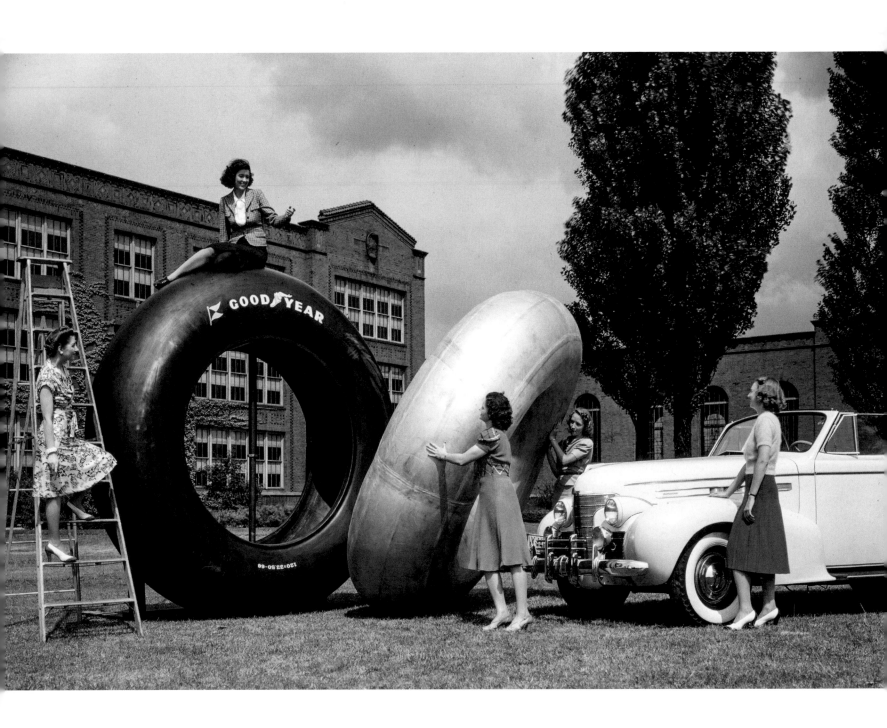

OHIO Women pose with rubber tires—each 10 feet (3 m) in diameter and weighing 700 pounds (318 kg)—made for a polar snow cruiser used for the 1939 to 1941 U.S. Antarctic Expedition led by Rear Admiral Richard E. Byrd. *Willard Culver, 1940*

MISSOURI After a day spent riding in St. Joe State Park, an all-terrain vehicle driver is covered in mud. *Randy Olson, 1996*

OHIO American soldiers stand in formation to fold the Stars and Stripes during the flag presentation at the 2012 Memorial Golf Tournament, founded by Jack Nicklaus, in Dublin, Ohio. *Jim Mandeville, 2012*

PEGGY WHITSON

"To Be of the Earth" was a poem I wrote as a kid. For me those words describe rolling hillsides of corn and soybeans that make up Iowa. Black Angus leisurely grazing the pastures of timothy and clover, calves frolicking beside. A life, and a way of life, that nurtured and supported my dreams.

Peggy Whitson is a retired NASA astronaut who participated in 10 space walks, more than any woman in the world. An Iowa native, she accumulated a total of 665 days in space over three long-duration missions—the most for any U.S. astronaut and more than any woman in the world. She was also the first female commander of the International Space Station and first female and nonmilitary chief of the Astronaut Office.

MISSOURI Technicians at the McDonnell Aircraft Corporation in St. Louis work on the nose of a Gemini capsule. NASA's Project Gemini aimed to test the human capacity for long-duration space-flights. Astronauts Buzz Aldrin and Jim Lovell made the final Gemini mission in November 1966. *James P. Blair, 1963*

OPPOSITE: INDIANA A lifeguard house illuminates the empty expanse of sand on a public Lake Michigan beach. *Robb Kendrick, 2011*

PAGE 372: KANSAS Newlyweds Darren and Jill Hodgkinson hold hands across a road north of Tipton, where they were married six hours earlier. *Joel Sartore, 1990*

PAGE 373: MICHIGAN A Muslim couple celebrates their wedding at the Islamic Center of America in Dearborn, which has one of the largest Muslim populations of any city in the United States. *Wayne Lawrence, 2017*

NORTH DAKOTA A black-tailed prairie dog (*Cynomys ludovicianus*) stands alert near the entrance to its burrow in Theodore Roosevelt National Park. *Dominique Braud, 2013*

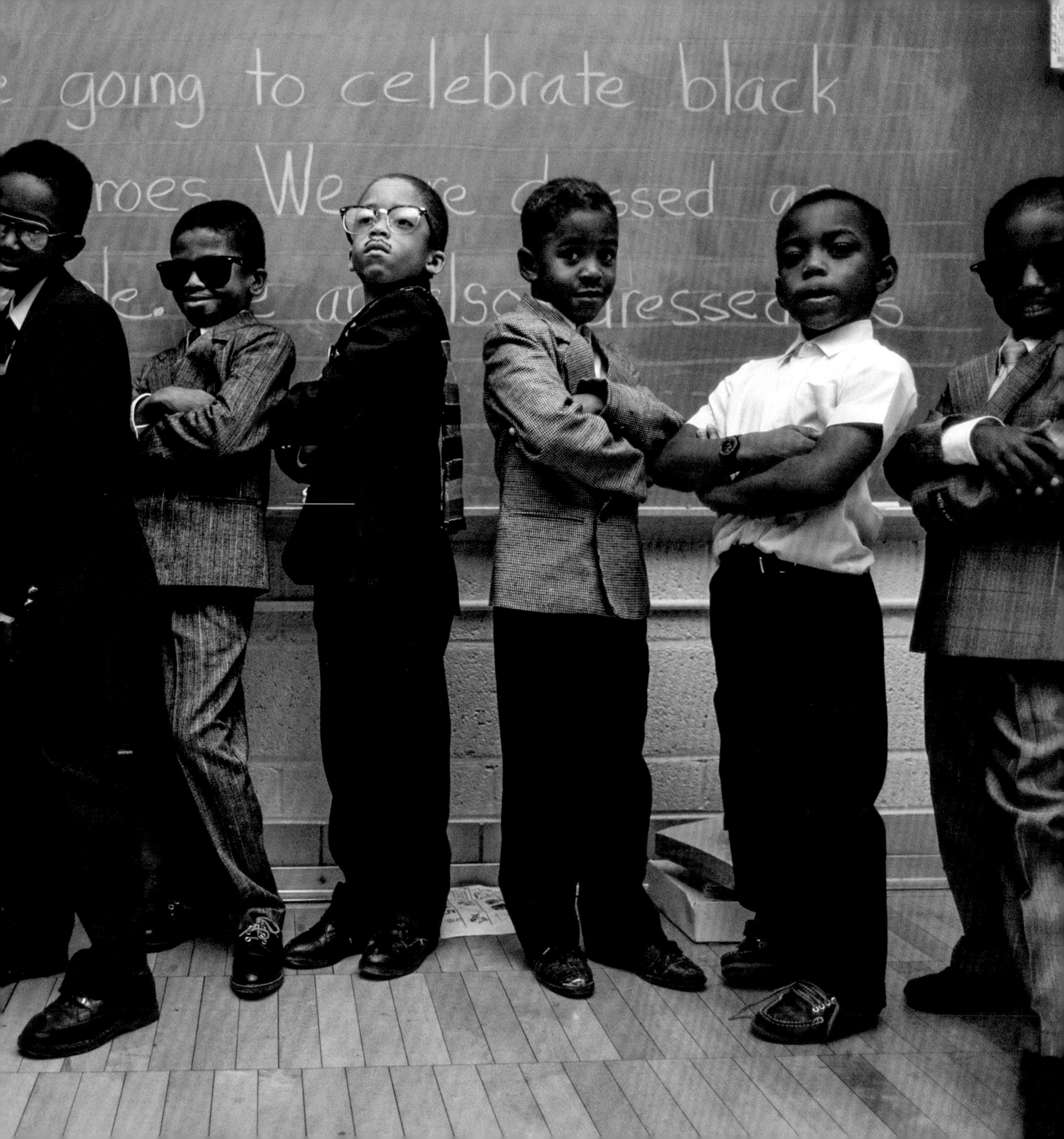
going to celebrate black

JAMES EARL JONES

For many, Michigan means lakes and football, icy cold winters bundled up or summers spent hanging out on hot city streets. Or for me, time spent in church with my grandparents or on stage at a school theater reciting lines. But we know Michigan is really about the people with big open hearts, like the kind teacher who taught me to stand up and speak. Michigan is a place where a young boy can find his true voice.

James Earl Jones is an Oscar-, Golden Globe-, Grammy-, and Tony Award-winning film and stage actor. He was born in Arkabutla, Mississippi, but raised in Brethren, Michigan; he graduated from the University of Michigan School of Music, Theatre & Dance in 1955.

MICHIGAN First graders dress as historical figures to celebrate Heritage Day and honor black American heroes at the Malcolm X Academy in Detroit. *George Steinmetz, 2011*

WISCONSIN On a Lake Michigan shore, rocks are encased in wintry ice and drip with icicles. *Bob Israel, 2010*

SOUTH DAKOTA A group of pronghorns relax in Buffalo Gap National Grassland. There are approximately 700,000 American pronghorns in the wild. *Annie Griffiths, 2004*

365

RONDA ROUSEY

My first memories are of wide-open spaces, huge skies, and 360 degrees of prairie surrounding my home. I remember bathing in murky well water and my wet hair freezing into icicles running to the car to go to school in the morning. My dad and I would jump in his car and just drive—not on any road but across the vast plains and little hills in whatever direction we pleased. We left more than just tire tracks; pieces of my heart will always be strewn across those amber waves of grain in North Dakota.

Ronda Rousey is a women's mixed martial arts (MMA) fighter; she has never lost a match since her amateur debut in 2010. A professional wrestler, actress, and author, she was the youngest judoka to qualify for the 2004 Olympic Games in Athens. She was raised in Jamestown, North Dakota.

NORTH DAKOTA Fog rolls over the sweeping landscape of Theodore Roosevelt National Park, which protects 70,448 acres (28,509.3 ha). Once President Roosevelt's bison hunting grounds, the area was added to the park system in 1978. *Mark Newman, 2016*

OHIO Amish women watch a professional harness racer blow past on the Geauga County fairground's half-mile (0.8 km) track. Men from their community participate in the high-wheel-cart challenge on the same track. *Randy Olson, 1997*

OHIO Taking a break from the Twins Days Festival, sisters have a laugh on the stairs outside the annual Twinsburg, Ohio, event. *Jodi Cobb, 2010*

NEBRASKA Sandhills Museum owner G. M. Sawyer relaxes outside with his mandolin. Sawyer gave up ranching to collect objects, including the pre-1928 cars, antique firearms and farm equipment, and moonshine stills on display at the museum. *Jodi Cobb, 1978*

DANNY PUDI

Illinois may be a very flat place in the middle of the country—but from here, you can go anywhere. This state produced multiple presidents and magnificent architecture, from Frank Lloyd Wright's buildings to the Sears Tower to the beautiful but not edible Bean.

Each year I drive across the state, from the mighty Mississippi to my hometown of Chicago. It was in this city that my parents, one from rural Poland and one from rural India, met. Only here could a thriving community of Polish Americans live in such close proximity to the Little India community on Devon Avenue. A person like me is only possible because of a place like this, because of Illinois.

Actor and comedian Danny Pudi was nominated three times for a Critics' Choice Award for his role as Abed Nadir on the hit show Community. *Known for his work in films such as* Knights of Badassdom *and starring roles in television shows, including* Mythic Quest, *he has also appeared in the off-Broadway musical* FOUND. *He was born in Brighton Park on Chicago's South Side.*

ILLINOIS An antenna serviceman sits atop the 100-story, 1,499-foot-tall (457 m) 875 North Michigan Avenue (formerly the John Hancock Center), working high above Chicago's other skyscrapers. *Lynn Johnson, 1989*

OPPOSITE: SOUTH DAKOTA The striated Brule Formation throughout Badlands National Park was deposited 30 to 34 million years ago and was shaped by ancient rivers flowing from the Black Hills. *Gerry Ellis, 2008*

PAGE 354: NORTH DAKOTA There are more than 480,000 acres (194,250 ha) of sunflower fields in North Dakota. Throughout the state, their golden petals bloom in abundance from early to mid August. *Darlyne A. Murawski, 2001*

PAGE 355: OHIO A man assembles an energy-efficient jet engine at the Peebles Test Operations General Electric Aviation Division, which tests more than 1,600 engines every year. *Tyrone Turner, 2009*

KIMORA LEE SIMMONS

Florissant, Missouri, is a working-class suburb north of St. Louis that I called home in the 1980s, along with many other minorities who migrated from the city center in hopes of opportunity: jobs, housing, something "more." I was mixed race, the daughter of a government-employed Korean immigrant. The community didn't know what to do with someone who looked like me—tall and gangly with *blasian** features—which impacted my confidence. My mom enrolled me in modeling classes to learn poise and presence. She, like so many others in the community, wanted more for her child. High fashion felt a million miles away from the working-class existence that surrounded me. Now, I see that it was exactly that community that motivated me to migrate toward opportunities of my own—to the catwalks of Paris, Milan, and New York. I look back at Florissant and realize we are all trying to move toward something more.

*Black and Asian

Kimora Lee Simmons is a Tony Award winner, entrepreneur, fashion designer, model, author, and philanthropist. She is also the Global Ambassador to The Unmentionables for the UN, committed to protecting refugees from exploitation and trafficking. She was raised in Florissant, Missouri, before beginning her modeling career at 13.

MISSOURI The Eads Bridge—a combined road and railway route connecting St. Louis, Missouri, and East St. Louis, Illinois—frames the Gateway Arch, a monument built to symbolize westward expansion, and the Mississippi River below. *Michael S. Lewis, 2004*

NORTH DAKOTA Blue sky shines through an open window of what remains of the abandoned Glucksdahl Lutheran Church. *Pete Ryan, 2006*

MICHIGAN Towering above the water and more than 50 feet (15 m) wide, Arch Rock is Mackinac Island's most famous rock formation. *Richard Nowitz, 2006*

SOUTH DAKOTA With the reverence accorded a sacred being, Oglala men carry a specially chosen cottonwood tree to the center of a Sun Dance circle. The tree will be the focus of a days-long spiritual ceremony. *Aaron Huey, 2012*

MISSOURI Two Santas chat after the Parade of Red Suits, part of Discover Santa, an annual convention held in Branson, where up to 750 professional Santas gather to hone their skills. *Dina Litovsky, 2016*

BOB BALLARD

When we sing of "amber waves of grain," or "somewhere over the rainbow," that's Kansas. To me, this great state personifies what being an American is all about. In fact, it brings a smile to my Kansan face when someone says that I'm "as corny as Kansas in August" and "high as a flag on the Fourth of July."

Robert Ballard is a retired U.S. Navy officer and professor of oceanography at the University of Rhode Island. Most famously, during work in underwater archaeology, he discovered the Titanic. He was raised in Wichita, Kansas.

KANSAS A double rainbow forms over a wheat field after a passing storm. *Mike Theiss, 2011*

OPPOSITE: SOUTH DAKOTA A couple in motorcycle attire watch a concert at the "Buffalo Chip" during the Sturgis Motorcycle Rally, which has been held for 80 years. *Aaron Huey, 2008*

PAGE 340: SOUTH DAKOTA It took nearly 400 men and women from October 1927 to October 1941 to carve the presidential faces into Mount Rushmore. Workers had to climb 700 stairs to the top of the mountain and were lowered to its face by ⅜-inch-thick steel cables. *Charles D'Emery, 1937*

PAGE 341: MINNESOTA Newborn piglets snuggle close together for a nap at the Minnesota State Fair's Miracle of Birth Center. The center exhibits 200 calves, lambs, goats, and piglets during the 12-day fair. *David Guttenfelder, 2019*

ANN BANCROFT

I grew up in the outskirts of Minneapolis/St. Paul, in an old, small farmhouse beside an apple orchard. In the winter, my parents would listen to jazz and noodle on a crossword puzzle in front of the fire. Outside our front door, a world of adventure awaited me. I learned to ice climb in our waterfall and started winter camping out back as an eight-year-old. My father would strap on his old wooden downhill skis and we'd sidestep up an enormous hill to pack down the snow. We'd work for hours to make the best sledding hill ever. Fond memories were made helping my dad fix our mile-long gravel road, feed our animals, or shovel snow.

Minnesotans are a hearty, positive people. We ice fish, build snow forts, or dogsled. This is a place that for me is about being physical, being outside. Minnesota fostered the things that I do today. It's here I learned a sense of love and wonderment.

Ann Bancroft is the first woman to travel across the ice at both the North and South Poles, the first woman to travel east to west across Greenland on skis, the leader of the American Women's Expedition that skied more than 600 miles (965.6 km) to the South Pole, and one of the first women to ski across Antarctica's landmass. A polar explorer and educator, she was raised in Minnesota, where she still lives.

MINNESOTA Celebrating an even heavier-than-usual snow year, a snowshoer throws flakes into the air. *Chris Gibbs, 2008*

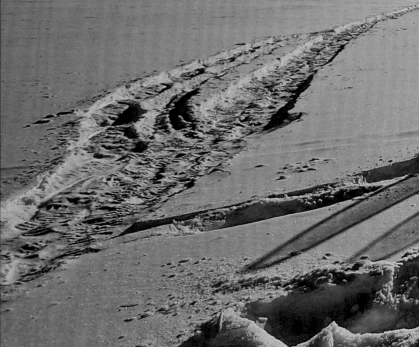

MICHIGAN Once a 1920s Hi-Speed gas station, Mr. Fix It on 8 Mile Road in Detroit is now an auto-repair shop. A sign painter named Eugene decorated the art deco building in his signature style. *George Steinmetz, 1992*

INDIANA Truck driver Larry King, from West Virginia, sits to get his boots shined at a truck stop in Fremont, Indiana. *National Geographic* called truck drivers "the new American cowboy" at the time of this photograph. *Tomasz Tomaszewski, 1988*

ILLINOIS Children cluster together to share the spray of a fountain in Chicago's Millennium Park. *Nikola Zlatkovic, 2010*

KANSAS Combines move across the fields, harvesting wheat from a farm. *George Steinmetz, 2013*

JOHN MELLENCAMP

Growing up in Indiana in the fifties and sixties was fantastic—a Norman Rockwell painting come to life, if you will. On Friday nights, my grandparents would take me to downtown Seymour, where people gathered and sold their farm products and shopped—all were local merchants, there were no box stores back then. It seemed as if my grandparents knew practically everyone in town. As a young child, I felt safe and secure.

As I entered my teenage years, it got even better: There was plenty of time for mischief and trouble if that's what you were looking for, and I was. There were only eight cops in the whole town to patrol 18,000 people. There was just me and James Dean on our 305 Scramblers. I used to lean on the parking meters and watch the girls drive by; some nights I even made it into their cars. At night, you could pick up radio stations from all over the country, and it made me feel like I was connected to the world. What a way to grow up in a small town.

John Mellencamp was born and raised in Seymour, Indiana. A musician, singer, songwriter, painter, and actor, he is best known for his hit singles "Hurts So Good," "Jack & Diane," "Small Town," and "R.O.C.K. in the U.S.A." He was inducted into the Rock and Roll Hall of Fame in 2008.

INDIANA Just outside Bloomington City Hall, a student violinist entertains shoppers at the Bloomington Farmers Market, a weekly gathering of farmers, growers, and producers selling their goods. *Steve Raymer, 2012*

KANSAS Two greater prairie chickens fight in a field near Flint Hills. The male birds typically battle for access to "booming" (or mating) grounds and, subsequently, females. *Michael Forsberg, 2006*

327

NEBRASKA Every year, up to 600,000 sandhill cranes migrate to the Platte River. They feast on food from nearby cornfields before returning to their Arctic and subarctic nesting grounds. *Andrew Coleman, 2018*

WISCONSIN Pilots fly restored World War II fighter planes—a Curtiss P-40E wearing the Flying Tigers insignia and a General Motors FM-2 Wildcat—during an air show. *Dale Gustafson, 1979*

WISCONSIN The ice caves of Apostle Islands National Lakeshore on Lake Superior are usually not accessible until February or March, when temperatures warm. *Susan Dykstra, 2016*

LAND OF HEART

ILLINOIS I INDIANA I IOWA I KANSAS I MICHIGAN I MINNESOTA I MISSOURI I NEBRASKA I NORTH DAKOTA I OHIO I SOUTH DAKOTA I WISCONSIN

For Katharine Bates, the alabaster city was a display at the 1893 World's Fair, located in Chicago, commerce's crossroads. There, electricity—the newly tamed mode of power—illuminated fairways at the famous flick of a switch, a symbol of progress and industry.

Beyond the city lights, the landscapes of the Midwest and plains weather through freezing cold, through mud and drought and threatening tornadoes, and yet they continue to inspire us. Deep snow and foot-thick ice across any one of these Great Lakes are taken as opportunities for sport and celebration. A chunky sunflower shyly opens, bright yellow petals greeting the season one by one. Hay furrows stretch farther than the eye can see. From above, the shapes of acres cultivated year after year appear as artful crescents and comely curves. Here in the Midwest, there are places where the far horizon stretches out so flat, you can see a rainbow in its entirety, end to end, a perfect arc echoed in St. Louis's Gateway Arch, designed to represent this midland's stretch to the West.

And here, you can still find iconic American charm. Newlyweds, whether dressed in gauzy frills and a cocky Stetson or in gilt embroidery and velvet slippers, declare with clasped hands the same commitment to love and cherish. High school football players bow their heads in prayer, pageant queens are named at county fairs, children rejoice in the spray of a fountain or the warmth of a new puppy.

In this place, visionary artists and engineers saw great faces in the rock, and revealed them over many years, one dynamite blast, one chip of a chisel at a time. A dozen Oglala men work together to carry the carefully selected cottonwood tree chosen for their ceremony. Many hands make light work in the heart of America.

OPPOSITE: KANSAS Those in the heartland learn to watch the skies for quickly changing weather. In Hays, a funnel cloud forms behind a windmill. *Keith Ladzinski, 2017*

PAGES 318-319: ILLINOIS Chicago's lights—mostly those of the city's streetlamps—burn bright under a blanket of clouds. *Jim Richardson, 2008*

CENTRAL PLAINS

O BEAUTIFUL FOR PATRIOT DREAM
THAT SEES BEYOND THE YEARS,
THINE ALABASTER CITIES GLEAM
UNDIMMED BY HUMAN TEARS!

CHAPTER FOUR

THE MIDWEST &

TEXAS A young boy sits on top of a car at Cadillac Ranch. The Amarillo, Texas, public art installation by Chip Lord, Hudson Marquez, and Doug Michels features 10 brightly painted 1949–1963 Cadillacs standing in the ground. *Tino Soriano, 2004*

DARIUS RUCKER

People ask why I still live in South Carolina, and I tell them all they need to do is visit to understand. Charleston is my hometown and my favorite place in the world. The city—and the state as a whole—is filled with genuine people and a laid-back energy that I love. Columbia will always be special to me, too. I met my Hootie & the Blowfish bandmates there when we were students together at University of South Carolina, and I still go back every chance I get to watch the Gamecocks play. To top it all off, South Carolina is full of amazing golf courses, incredible beaches, and delicious low country cooking—some of my favorite things!

Darius Rucker is a country singer and the lead vocalist and rhythm guitarist of rock band Hootie & the Blowfish, which he founded with his bandmates in 1986 at the University of South Carolina. He was born and raised in Charleston.

SOUTH CAROLINA Sailors push their vessel toward the ocean as beachgoers walk by on Hilton Head Island. *Kenneth Garrett, 2006*

OPPOSITE: **MISSISSIPPI** A beautiful driveway in Vicksburg is bordered by moss-covered trees and purple flowering bushes. *Sam Abell, 1996*

PAGE 312: **ALABAMA** Palmettos meet the sun in Bon Secour National Wildlife Refuge, some of Alabama's last remaining undisturbed coastal barrier habitat. *Raymond Gehman, 2000*

PAGE 313: **OKLAHOMA** Windmills glisten in a twilight sky in Stillwater. *Emory Kristof, 2001*

ROY WOOD, JR.

Alabama is a place of complicated optimism. It's a beautiful place with beautiful people. As a kid, I used to play baseball and deliver pizzas, then I started delivering rib eye steaks door-to-door in the more wealthy neighborhoods. That's when I saw the wealth gap. Once I started doing stand-up comedy, I got beyond Birmingham, to see the mountains and the beaches, the green peaks and valleys. But, it's more than that. They say Alabama's two main exports are football and racism. That's not all true. This is a place of redemption and growth. In Huntsville, we make rockets. I filmed a sitcom television show there. Montgomery, a city wrought with civil rights issues, recently elected their first black mayor. That's progress, that's growth and change. It's a place that's evolving and maturing. I'm very, very proud to be from Alabama.

Roy Wood, Jr., is a comedian and actor who has entertained millions across stage, television, and radio. He joined The Daily Show with Trevor Noah *as a correspondent in 2015, and in 2017 was named the new host of Comedy Central's storytelling series,* This Is Not Happening. *His one-hour stand-up special,* Roy Wood, Jr.: No One Loves You, *premiered in 2019. Wood is a native of Birmingham, Alabama.*

ALABAMA In the Avondale neighborhood of Birmingham, Bottletree Café (closed in 2015) served vegan fare along with burgers, beer, and live music. *Susan Seubert, 2014*

OPPOSITE: **U.S. VIRGIN ISLANDS** A small school of adult palometa fish dodge the feet of a St. John visitor. *David Doubilet, 1994*

PAGE 306: **MISSISSIPPI** University of Mississippi senior Alexis Cassidy Burdine, 21, poses at Isom Place, an antebellum mansion in Oxford. *William Albert Allard, 1989*

PAGE 307: **OKLAHOMA** In 2012, then 88-year-old K'asA Henry Washburn was one of only four fluent speakers of Euchee left and had been called a "living dictionary." He taught children their native tongue at the Euchee Language House. *Lynn Johnson, 2012*

TED TURNER

My lifelong love of nature was firmly planted in me at a very young age and grew stronger while learning to sail as an adolescent along Savannah's beautiful marsh waters. As a young man in advertising and, later, cable, I was gripped by Atlanta: a city ripe for change and ready for a place on the global stage. Over the years, my family and I have enjoyed Georgia's mountains and natural landscapes as much as its bustling capital city. The state of Georgia continues to hold special meaning to me and will always be where I call home.

Cable pioneer, champion sailor, philanthropist, and conservationist Ted Turner has dedicated the latter decades of his life to global causes, such as the environment, species conservation, and nuclear weapons nonproliferation. Today, Turner retains the world's largest private herd of bison across his two million acres (809,371.3 ha) of land, located in nine states as well as Argentina. His focus remains on the work of his five foundations—including the United Nations Foundation, Nuclear Threat Initiative, and Turner Foundation—as well as his businesses, including Turner Enterprises, Ted's Montana Grill restaurants, and Ted Turner Reserves.

GEORGIA The skyscrapers of downtown Atlanta tower over Centennial Olympic Park. *Richard Nowitz, 2013*

OPPOSITE: **TEXAS** El Paso third baseman Greg Edge bows his head for the playing of "The Star-Spangled Banner" before a minor-league game against Midland. *William Albert Allard, 1991*

PAGE 300: **PUERTO RICO** A Puerto Rican debutante of Castilian descent poses for a picture. *Charles Martin, 1924*

PAGE 301: **SOUTH CAROLINA** Built in 1763 by John Rutledge, a noted signer of the U.S. Constitution, the John Rutledge House Inn is now a historic landmark—and is still open for business. *Michael George, 2019*

WAYNE BRADY

My favorite childhood memory is traveling to St. Thomas, U.S. Virgin Islands, with my grandmother to visit family. I've been going there since I was kid, eating johnnycakes, playing on the beach. I have a ton of cousins and aunts there. I was born in Georgia, raised in Florida, but my soul is from the Virgin Islands. It's in me. My drive, my hustle, my art, my work ethic. I'm so proud to have that USVI connection. In my heart, St. Thomas is where I'm from. My grandmother, my father, my aunts are from there. This is what's inside of me. What gives me the power, drive, and strength to go forward. It's because of the island blood of St. Thomas, St. Croix, and St. John in me that I do what I do. It's the work ethic. It's how I was raised.

Wayne Brady is a multiple Emmy Award–winning actor and comedian. His career took off with Whose Line Is It Anyway? *and segued into appearances on Broadway, a Grammy Award–nominated R & B single, and films including* Crossover *and* Roll Bounce. *Raised in Orlando, Florida, he has family roots in the Virgin Islands.*

U.S. VIRGIN ISLANDS The friendly St. John town of Coral Bay sits above Coral Harbor and offers white-sand beaches and sparkling Caribbean waters. *Hannele Lahti, 2006*

LOUISIANA Spanish moss covers an old cypress tree growing from Lake Verret in the Atchafalaya National Wildlife Refuge. The refuge aims to protect habitats of neotropical songbirds, Louisiana black bears, waterfowl, and other native species. *Yva Momatiuk and John Eastcott, 1979*

NORTH CAROLINA Stained glass ornaments decorate a street-facing shop window on Ocracoke Island in Cape Hatteras National Seashore. *Stephen St. John, 2014*

LOUISIANA A member of the 7th Ward Creole Hunters—one of about 38 tribes of the Mardi Gras Indian Nation—parades through the city during New Orleans Jazz Fest. *Greg Davis, 2013*

MARY STEENBURGEN

I am made of Arkansas. It raised me, for better or worse: chicken and dumplings; walking to church; seeing injustice and the need to fight against it; the sound of my freight train conductor daddy's trains; being inspired by brilliant public school teachers; chasing lightning bugs at dusk; protesting a war; being taught what love was by not just my parents, but by a community; reveling in the beauty of its woods and waters; drill team on Friday nights; listening to Bobby Blue Bland at Hank's Dog House; being raised around world-class senses of humor; and learning, in the hard times, how big the hearts of Arkansans are. It is the birth of all of my dreams, and it gave me the push to go after them. I feel blessed to be from Arkansas.

Mary Steenburgen is an Academy Award– and Golden Globe–winning actress known for her work in films such as Book Club, Melvin and Howard, *and* Time After Time *and the television shows* Zoey's Extraordinary Playlist *and* The Last Man on Earth. *A songwriter for Warner Chappell, Mary co-wrote the Critics' Choice– and Hollywood Critics Association–winning song "Glasgow (No Place Like Home)," which was shortlisted for an Academy Award. She was raised in North Little Rock, Arkansas.*

ARKANSAS Railroad tracks run along the top of a river levee above the Arkansas Delta and Mississippi River floodplain. *Nathan Benn, 1983*

GEORGIA Making for a novel wedding reception, Annette Solomon and her husband, Godfrey, join Atlanta's Fourth of July parade, dancing to calypso music—a nod to the groom's native Trinidad—down Peachtree Street. *Jim Richardson, 1988*

TEXAS NASA astronaut Suni Williams has served two stints on the International Space Station, culminating in 322 days spent in space. She took a copy of the Bhagavad Gita, as well as a figurine and picture of Ganesha, on her first trip. *Ismail Ferdous, 2018*

CARY FOWLER

One way to look at Tennessee is to notice how it stretches from the Smokies to the Mississippi with reverential stops for country, blues, and rock-and-roll music; barbecue; Civil War battlefields; and civil rights memorials. For me, Tennessee's more personal: lessons in integrity from my father the judge, learning an appreciation for good food from my mother the dietician, and an awakening to the larger world while at picturesque Rhodes College. But it was my grandmother who introduced me to my life's work on our fifth-generation family farm in Madison County. Groomed to be a farmer, I instead got stuck on seeds.

Cary Fowler is perhaps best known as the "father" of the Svalbard Global Seed Vault. An agriculturalist and former executive director for the Global Crop Diversity Trust, he is the author of Seeds on Ice: Svalbard and the Global Seed Vault *and a recipient of numerous awards. He was raised in Tennessee and attended Rhodes College in Memphis.*

TENNESSEE A combine harvester is used to efficiently harvest grains in western Tennessee. *Karen Kasmauski, 2009*

MISSISSIPPI Modeling trendy styles from the 1980s, a couple takes a stroll in Oxford, Mississippi. *William Albert Allard, 1986*

SOUTH CAROLINA A group of paddlers link up their canoes in Congaree National Park, which encompasses bottomland hardwood forest and the Congaree and Wateree Rivers. *Corey Arnold, 2016*

FLORIDA Bundled newborns are arranged for a portrait at Orlando's Winnie Palmer Hospital, the second busiest birth facility in the United States at the time of this photograph. *John Stanmeyer, 2011*

EVA LONGORIA

In this one expansive state, there are the surfers in a sparkling city by the sea; the big, bustling cities of Houston and Dallas; the border; and the place most important to me, our ranch.

Here, in land granted to my family in 1603, my sisters and I would rise early, grab a tortilla, and spend the day running through the woods. Dad worked the cattle, pigs, and chickens and grew crops of corn or watermelon. We girls would run. No other neighbor or house in sight. Just quiet. We'd watch a storm roll in. And on a clear night, climb to our roof to gaze at all the stars. In Texas, I learned to read the big sky.

This is the land built by generations of Spanish explorers, indigenous tribes, Tejanos, and Irish. Sometimes we forget these brave, ambitious people are what made us strong. They are what we celebrate. This is where I have my land, my roots. Texas is home.

Eva Longoria is an actress, producer, director, and activist. She is the founder of The Eva Longoria Foundation, which helps Latinas build better futures for themselves through education and entrepreneurship. She was raised on a ranch near Corpus Christi, Texas, and received her bachelor of science in kinesiology from Texas A&M University-Kingsville.

TEXAS Mexican-American students at Robert L. Martin School in Brownsville stand to say the Pledge of Allegiance. This photo was originally published in *National Geographic* as part of a story about the 1981 Supreme Court ruling allowing children of undocumented immigrants to attend U.S. public schools. *Danny Lehman, 1985*

BENICIO DEL TORO

Puerto Rico is nature, the Atlantic Ocean and the Caribbean Sea, the lagoons and rivers, the mountains and forests, the palm trees and fruit trees, the coquí frog with its eternal melancholy song, and the Puerto Rican parrots struggling against extinction.

Puerto Rico is the history of the Taíno, Spain, Africa, Latin America, and of the United States of America. Puerto Rico is music, art, and literature. Puerto Rico is sports and Caribbean cuisine. Puerto Rico is its flag: blue, white, and red with a lone star.

Puerto Rico is its people and their warmth, their sense of humor, and their resilience. Puerto Rico is my family and my loved ones, who have lived their lives there and taught me through words and action how to love my island and its culture.

Benicio del Toro was born and raised in Puerto Rico until the age of 15, when he moved with his family to Pennsylvania. A critically acclaimed actor, he won an Academy Award, British Academy of Film and Television Arts Award, Golden Globe, and Screen Actors Guild Award for his role in the film Traffic. *His body of work also includes* Escobar: Paradise Lost, Che, Sicario, *and* Star Wars: The Last Jedi.

PUERTO RICO A woman shows off her sequined Puerto Rican flag dress at the annual Carnaval de Ponce, a weeklong celebration held before the beginning of Lent since the first half of the 19th century. *Amy Toensing, 2003*

ARKANSAS Farmers work to harvest cabbage in Newport.
Bill Barksdale, 2016

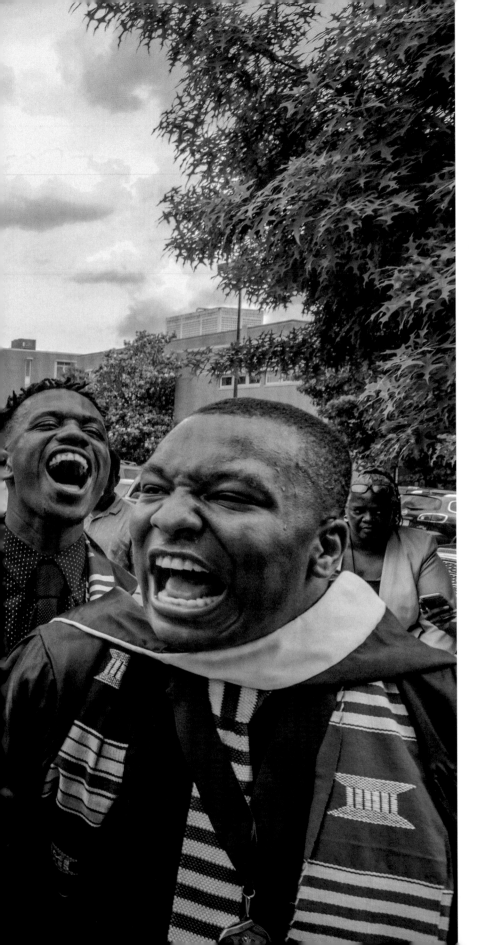

GEORGIA Members of the Sigma Pi Phi fraternity celebrate their graduation from Morehouse College, a historically black, all-male school. The college was first established as the August Institute just two years after the Civil War, and later the Atlanta Baptist Seminary when it moved to the city in 1879. *Ruddy Roye, 2017*

N. SCOTT MOMADAY

I believe that place is a crucial factor in the determination of our human being. As a member of the Kiowa tribe of Oklahoma, I am at home in the Southern Plains. Much of my writing has centered upon that powerful and sacred landscape. When I think of the deep spirit of America, I think of Oklahoma. It is my place of inspiration and belonging.

N. Scott Momaday, a Kiowa Indian, was born in Lawton, Oklahoma. A multiple award-winning author and poet, he won the Pulitzer Prize for Fiction for his first novel, House Made of Dawn. Momaday was a founding trustee of the National Museum of the American Indian and is the Regents Professor of the Humanities at the University of Arizona.

OKLAHOMA The sun rises above the Great Plains outside the city of Antlers.
Jack Rogers, 2011

KENTUCKY A guide addresses Boy Scouts from Booth's Amphitheater in Mammoth Cave. Mammoth is the largest known cave system in the world, carved more than 10 million years ago and first explored by humans in 400 B.C. *David S. Boyer and Arlan R. Wiker, 1964*

PUERTO RICO Cueva Ventana sits on top of a limestone cliff in Arecibo and overlooks the Río Grande de Arecibo and valley below. *Stephen Alvarez, 2014*

PUERTO RICO A rocky beach meets ancient walls lining the shores of Old San Juan. *Ira Block, 2004*

ROBIN ROBERTS

In Mississippi, the Gulf Coast is majestic and serene, the food is fried, and warmth is everywhere. I don't mean just the weather, but there's warmth in the music of the blues, in the soul service gospel I heard at my church as a child, and in the people. When you see someone in Pass Christian, the quintessential small town where I grew up, you stop and wave. New to town? A neighbor will bring a Bundt cake. That's just what you do.

We were a military family, and I grew up moving all the time. But when it came time for my father to retire from the U.S. Air Force, the Roberts family got to decide where we would put down our roots. I am proud to say we chose Mississippi. It is home.

Robin Roberts is the anchor of ABC's Good Morning America *and host of "Thriver Thursday," which highlights people who persevere after life-altering circumstances. She was born in Tuskegee, Alabama, but was raised in Pass Christian, Mississippi.*

MISSISSIPPI Legendary guitarist, singer-songwriter, and producer B. B. King performs at a blues festival in Pickens. *William Albert Allard, 1999*

OPPOSITE: FLORIDA At sunrise, reeds are reflected in the water of Sweet Bay Pond, part of Everglades National Park. The Everglades are the only subtropical preserve in North America. *Tim Fitzharris, 2006*

PAGE 258: ALABAMA Technicians at the Marshall Space Flight Center work to complete the Saturn V launch vehicle, which was later used to launch Skylab, the first American space station. *James P. Blair, 1963*

PAGE 259: TENNESSEE The stools fronting the snack bar at Sun Studio—home of the "million-dollar quartet"—bear the names of the studio's famous recording artists, including Elvis Presley, Carl Perkins, and Johnny Cash. *Stephen St. John, 2012*

DALE EARNHARDT, JR.

North Carolina is where I learned about cars and how to race. Here, just east of the Great Smoky Mountains, is where my family has deep roots, and where my roots will always be, now that I have a family of my own. My race team is here, my family is here, and my life is here.

U.S. VIRGIN ISLANDS Tunicates, also known as sea squirts, cling to a coral overhang in Virgin Islands National Park, which occupies the majority of St. John. *David Doubilet, 1994*

ARKANSAS Inside the White River National Wildlife Refuge, a search team scans the forest and skies for ivory-billed woodpeckers. *Joel Sartore, 2006*

SOUTH CAROLINA Brown pelicans nest on Edisto Island's Deveaux Bank, a 215-acre (87 ha) bird sanctuary at the mouth of the North Edisto River. *Vincent J. Musi, 2012*

TENNESSEE The sunset at Newfound Gap casts the forest in Great Smoky Mountains National Park in shades of blue. *Michael Melford, 2005*

MICHAEL LEWIS

Someone once said that you can't understand New Orleans unless you stop thinking of it as the southernmost city in North America and start thinking of it as the northernmost city in South America. I grew up in Louisiana and have come to see it as an entirely in-between place—and not just geographically. Fly into it from the Gulf of Mexico, up the Mississippi River. Hundreds of square miles that are neither land nor water but something in between. It's also a place that has historically blurred language and identity: in between French and English. In between black and white. If you want clarity, go somewhere else. If you want a mixed drink, it's your place.

Michael Lewis has published a number of New York Times *bestselling books including* The Fifth Risk, The Undoing Project, *and* Flash Boys. *Three of his books—*The Big Short, The Blind Side, *and* Moneyball—*have been turned into Academy Award–nominated films. The creator of the podcast* Against the Rules, *he grew up in New Orleans and lives in Berkeley, California, with his wife and three children.*

LOUISIANA A statue of a black woman rises where one of Confederate president Jefferson Davis once stood in New Orleans. Film director Zac Manuel (center) used the statue in a music video for "If All I Was Was Black" by soul singer Mavis Staples. *Gillian Laub, 2018*

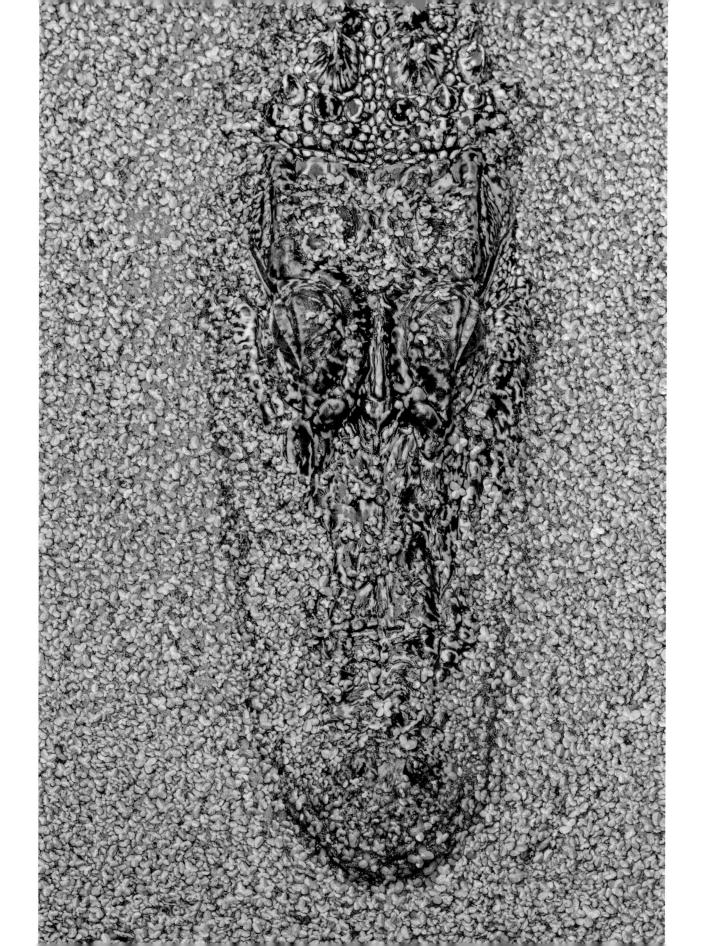

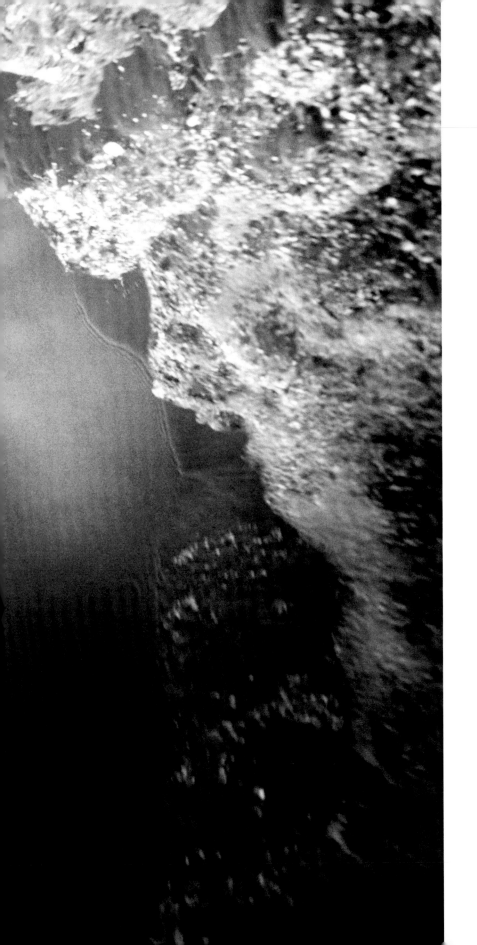

OPPOSITE: **NORTH CAROLINA** A young surfer cuts through a barrel wave formed off the Outer Banks. *Chris Bickford, 2011*

PAGE 244: **LOUISIANA** An American alligator *(Alligator mississippiensis)* surfaces amid duckweed. There are at least one million wild gators in Louisiana. *John Cancalosi, 2014*

PAGE 245: **TENNESSEE** Taylor Swift's Swarovski crystal-encrusted Taylor-brand guitar sits on display at Nashville's Country Music Hall of Fame and Museum. *Stephen St. John, 2013*

LORETTA LYNN

I was born in Van Lear, in eastern Kentucky. My family were all coal miners, farmers, and moonshiners. Eastern Kentucky is still one of the poorest areas in the state; we had very little growing up, but we never knew we were poor because up there, no one had much. Family was everything and music was ingrained in everyone there. Families would gather on porches and in church houses and schools to sing and play anything from fiddles to spoons to washboards. That was what we did for fun because it was all we could afford to do. If I hadn't come from those mountains, in those times, with those people, I don't think I would've ever become a singer, songwriter, or author. There's something about those mountains that roots itself within your bones. I am proud to be a coal miner's daughter and I am proud to be a Kentuckian.

Loretta Lynn is an award-winning country music singer and songwriter whose multiple-gold album career has spanned more than 60 years. She continues to tour and appear at the Grand Ole Opry in Nashville, Tennessee, where she became part of the music scene in the 1960s. She was raised in Van Lear, Kentucky.

KENTUCKY Banjo player Morgan Sexton made his first instrument from a lard bucket and bought his first real banjo at 17 for $10.86 from the Sears Roebuck catalog. Nearly 70 years later, in 1991, he won the National Endowment for the Arts' National Heritage Fellowship for his music. *Karen Kasmauski, 1992*

KENTUCKY There are only 20 registered pure white Thoroughbreds—like this mare and her foal on Patchen Wilkes Farm—in the United States. They get their rare color from a mutated gene known as KIT. *Melissa Farlow, 2003*

FLORIDA A manatee rests in the Weeki Wachee River. There are an estimated 6,500 manatees living around U.S. waters in Florida and Puerto Rico. *Brian Skerry, 2009*

ARKANSAS Peaty Moore takes his 11-year-old son, Drew, on an evening drive through the farmlands of their hometown of Wynne, Arkansas, where their family has lived for generations. They share a bond built on exploring the outdoors, hunting, and fishing. *Pete Muller, 2016*

CAUTION
Avoid Injury
From Fire
• Static electricity
may ignite fuel
vapors.
• Place fuel container
on ground when
filling.

TEXAS Rocks hang in the balance at Big Bend National Park, framing the Chihuahuan Desert and rocky peaks in the distance. *Andrew Coleman, 2019*

JIMMY BUFFETT

Saying what Florida means to me in a handful of words is not an easy task. Florida began with free orange juice at the welcome station on the Flora-Bama border. It blossomed in Key West, where I wrote a three-minute song that people liked, and I didn't have to get a day job.

Singer, songwriter, and author Jimmy Buffett is best known for his hits, such as "Margaritaville," "Cheeseburger in Paradise," and "Come Monday." He is a fourth-generation sailor and fisherman, a pilot, surfer, and frequent traveler to remote and exotic places of the world, having become addicted to National Geographic magazine as a child. Born in Mississippi, he has made Florida his home for years.

FLORIDA Enjoying the sand, beachgoers partake in a game of volleyball on half-mile-long (0.8 km) Smathers Beach, the largest public beach in Key West. *David Alan Harvey, 1981*

OKLAHOMA A rodeo clown in full makeup walks past competitors backstage at a rodeo event in Oklahoma City. *William Albert Allard, 1980*

MISSISSIPPI A man eats outside the Old Country Store in Lorman. A former general store built on a local plantation in 1875, the rustic building is now home to a gift shop, thrift store, and Mr. D's restaurant, serving "heavenly" fried chicken. *Randy Olson, 1998*

NORTH CAROLINA Early morning breakers crash into a pier jutting from Nags Head, a beach town in the Outer Banks. *David Alan Harvey, 1980*

229

LAND OF TRADITION

Pride is a word one frequently hears in the South. Pride in traditions, heritage, and America itself. Here, nature presents ideals of serenity—ridge upon ridge in the cool, gray Smoky Mountains, star-spangled skies over a Texas observatory, dawn-kissed swamps in the Everglades, moss-draped trees and azaleas lining the pathway home.

Yet nature isn't always easy. It can also throw many a challenge, too. Storm waves crash into a time-tested pier. A camouflaged alligator lurks beneath the duckweed. We come face-to-face with the dreaded rattler.

Just as we encounter the throes of the wild, here too, we come face-to-face with a history of hardship. It hasn't always been easy, living up to American ideals. When Katharine Bates wrote her poem in 1893, the "liberating strife" of the War Between the States was decades past, yet the struggle was far from over. Throughout this region we see signs of resilience through struggle. Witness the fortress walls of Old San Juan, built to take an onslaught centuries back and still standing. Mexican-American children raise the red, white, and blue and speak the words "I pledge allegiance." African-American college graduates cheer each other on, toppling old prejudices. Native American elders hold true to ancient tongues.

Here in the South and Caribbean, music and a sense of innovation has carried us through. This is the home of American greats: the birthplace of the blues, the banjo, rock-and-roll, jazz, stock car racing, rockets to the moon, the Derby. Elvis Presley and B.B. King. Dale Earnhardt, Jr., and Loretta Lynn. Icons and legends were born in these parts and American history made.

We still hear the story of the South in the strains of old-time fiddles, the yearning tales told in country music ballads. We sing and dance together. In these and countless other ways we see how a nation of many becomes one.

OPPOSITE: FLORIDA First Lady Claudia "Lady Bird" Johnson, President Lyndon B. Johnson, and Vice President Spiro T. Agnew joined 8,000 distinguished guests and 2,000 journalists to watch Apollo 11 lift off from the Kennedy Space Center on July 16, 1969. *Otis Imboden, 1969*

PAGES 224-225: LOUISIANA Azaleas bloom in front of a live oak tree in the Jungle Gardens—a 170-acre (69 ha) semitropical garden stretching along Bayou Petite Anse on Avery Island. *Diane Cook and Len Jenshel, 2015*

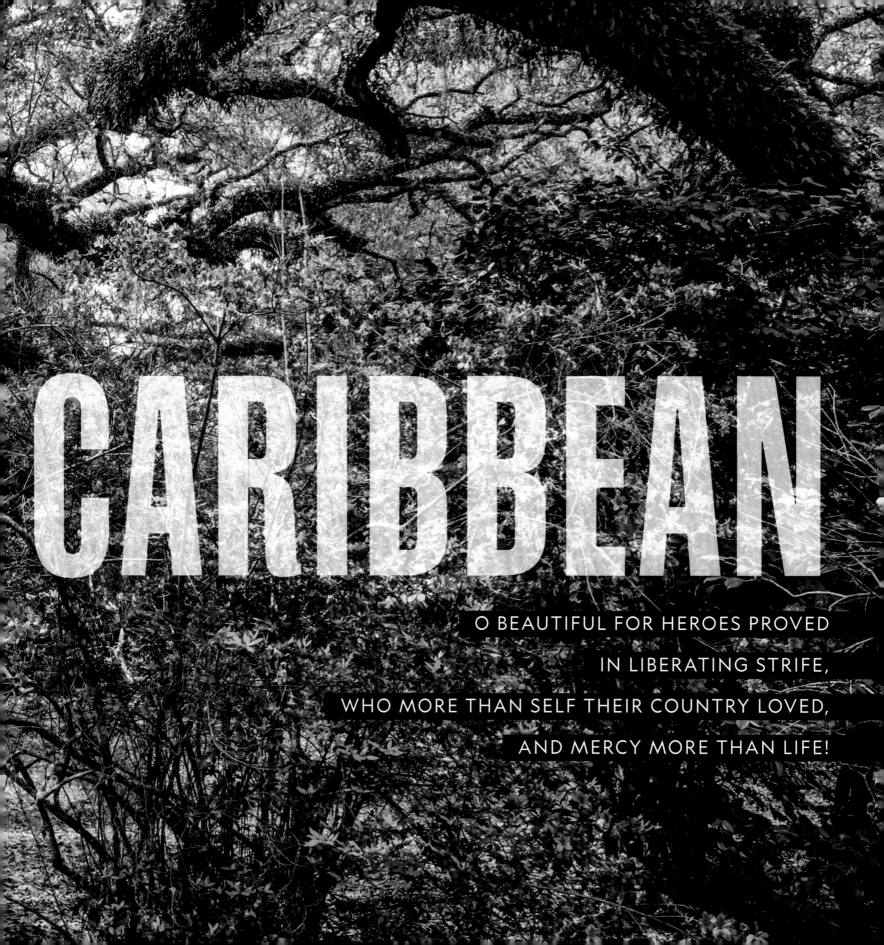

CARIBBEAN

O BEAUTIFUL FOR HEROES PROVED

IN LIBERATING STRIFE,

WHO MORE THAN SELF THEIR COUNTRY LOVED,

AND MERCY MORE THAN LIFE!

CHAPTER THREE

THE SOUTH &

MAINE A birch- and sedge-lined path is part of the 125-mile (201 km) network of hiking trails and 44 miles (71 km) of carriage roads available inside Acadia National Park, one of the smallest national parks in the country. *Michael Melford, 2005*

WEST VIRGINIA Dusty coal miners make their way down a road
in a coal camp after a day of work. *Volkmar Wentzel, 1938*

WEST VIRGINIA Appalachian Trail hikers pause on a footbridge in Harpers Ferry, West Virginia. *Robert Szabo, 2012*

WYLIE DUFRESNE

Almost every memory I have of my childhood in Rhode Island is tied to food: celery-salt dogs at Haven Brothers Diner, pickles from a barrel at my dad's sandwich shop, frozen lemonade from a Del's truck outside my school. It's where I tasted my first clam strip, bit into my first jelly stick doughnut, and drank my first coffee milk. When you grow up in the smallest state in the country, you have to appreciate the little things—and I did. I ate them up.

Wylie Dufresne is a leading proponent of molecular gastronomy, Michelin-starred chef, and James Beard Award winner. He is the chef and owner of Brooklyn, New York's Du's Donuts and Coffee, applying the imagination and inventive techniques to the craft his great-grandfather once practiced at Ever Good Donut Shop in Central Falls, Rhode Island. Previously, Dufresne was the chef and owner of wd-50 and Alder in New York City.

RHODE ISLAND Members of the Newport Rotary Club prepare a traditional New England feast of lobsters, clams, corn, and potatoes. The food is cooked in seaweed spread over heated stones, a technique English settlers learned from Native American tribes in the region. *Fred Ward, 1968*

PENNSYLVANIA On Philadelphia's 13th and Locust Streets, local artist Meg Saligman's "Philadelphia Muses," which she completed in 1999, depicts some of the city's performing artists. *Raymond Patrick, 2005*

MASSACHUSETTS Gray seals play in the waters off the sandy coast of Cape Cod. *Brian Skerry, 2014*

JOHN IRVING

My first job was picking apples in Hampton Falls, New Hampshire. From the taller trees, I could see the ocean. Or maybe I couldn't see the ocean, but I knew it was there. Now I live in Canada. When I see seagulls in Toronto, I remember the seagulls I saw in the apple orchards.

John Irving is the best-selling author of critically acclaimed novels including The World According to Garp, The Cider House Rules, *and* A Prayer for Owen Meany. *He was born in Exeter, New Hampshire, and graduated from the University of New Hampshire.*

NEW HAMPSHIRE A young girl bites into a caramel apple at the Sandwich Fair, which is held annually on Columbus Day weekend. *Heather Perry, 2004*

OPPOSITE: NEW YORK The American Falls is the second largest of the three waterfalls that collectively make up Niagara Falls. Niagara Falls State Park is the oldest state park in the country. *Mike Theiss, 2015*

PAGE 208: NEW HAMPSHIRE Approximately 2,340 wrap threads—nearly 6.5 miles (10.5 km) in total—are wound on a cylinder to start the run for 250 cotton blankets at the Nashua mills. *Willard Culver, 1941*

PAGE 209: NEW YORK Macy's employees steer Bullwinkle and Donald Duck floats down Manhattan's Central Park West as part of the two-mile-long (3 km) Macy's Thanksgiving Day Parade. *Albert Moldvay, 1964*

209

HANNAH TETER

The Green Mountain State attracts people from around the world with its neon colors every fall, and fills their bellies with maple syrup, cheddar cheese, and Ben & Jerry's. Vermont has the best of both worlds—mountains full of snow and beautiful lakes all around. Growing up on a mountaintop, my mom had a huge organic garden overly abundant with fruits and vegetables; the fertile Vermont soil and perfectly humid summer climate makes living off the land a little easier.

This is the birthplace of snowboarding, created here by Jake Burton. Vermont led the charge to a globally loved sport and Olympic dreams for many—including myself.

Hannah Teter is a world champion snowboarder and Olympic gold and silver medalist. Born to a family of snowboarders in Belmont, Vermont, she became the youngest member of the U.S. Snowboard Team in 2003 and made her Olympic debut in 2006. The winner of the ESPY Award for Best Female Action Sports Athlete, she is also a global ambassador for the Special Olympics.

VERMONT Ski lifts make their way up Madonna Mountain at Smugglers' Notch. The ski resort features 78 ski and snowboarding runs. *Tim Laman, 2007*

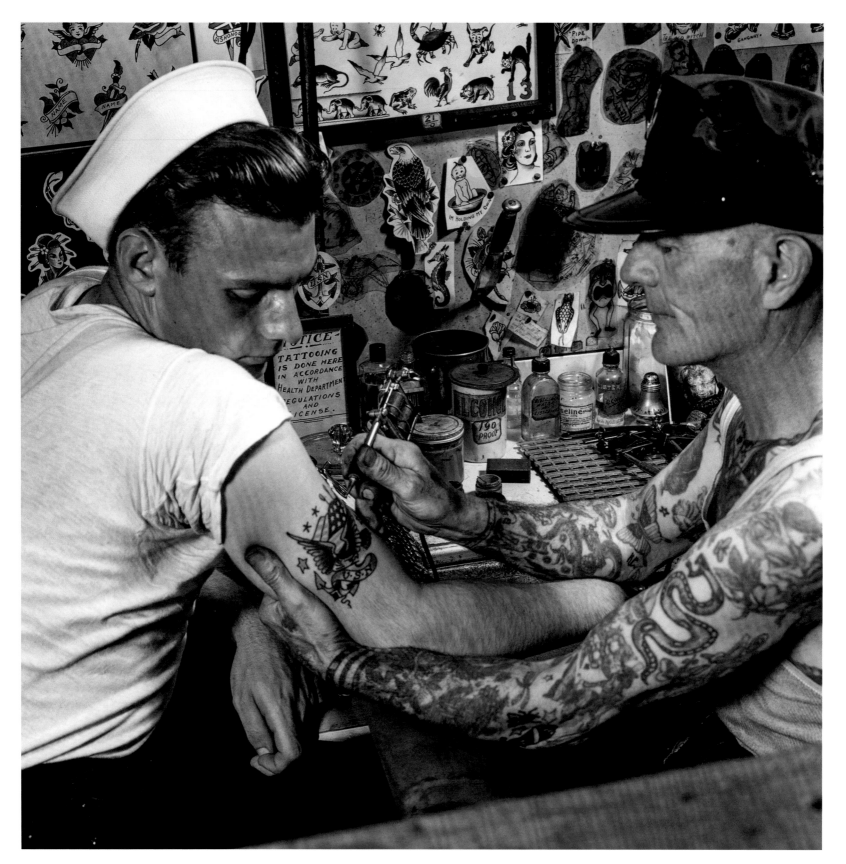

205

OPPOSITE: VIRGINIA A young red fox kit curiously picks his way through a backyard in suburban Manassas. *Hannele Lahti, 2006*

PAGE 204: MASSACHUSETTS On Memorial Day, 37,000 American flags decorate Boston Common, honoring military members who died in service from the Revolutionary War to the present day. *Babak Tafreshi, 2015*

PAGE 205: VIRGINIA A sailor gets tattooed with an eagle and the Stars and Stripes in Norfolk. *Paul L. Pryor, 1939*

CAL RIPKEN, JR.

When I think back on my playing career with the Baltimore Orioles, I consider myself one of the fortunate ones who had the chance to play their entire career with the hometown team.

There is so much to love about the Old Line State: steamed crabs and history—from the writing of our national anthem to Fort McHenry; great cities and waterfront communities; a world-class aquarium; and the finest education and health care institutions in the nation. Maryland is and always will be home—as the state's song says, "Maryland, My Maryland."

Cal Ripken, Jr., earned the nickname "The Iron Man" as a shortstop and third baseman for the Baltimore Orioles. After 21 seasons with the team, he became president and CEO of Ripken Baseball, Inc. He was inducted into the National Baseball Hall of Fame in 2007. Raised in Havre de Grace, Maryland, he now calls Annapolis home.

MARYLAND On a cold autumn morning, fishing boats dock near a crab shanty on Smith Island. *Shannon Hibberd, 2006*

NEW YORK As part of JR's Inside Out project, New Yorkers and visitors were asked to take self-portraits in Times Square at the site of the first ever photo booth almost 100 years ago. The resulting 6,000 images were pasted on Duffy Square. *Stephen Alvarez, 2013*

NEW JERSEY Ravi S. Bhalla, an Indian-American civil rights lawyer, became mayor of Hoboken in 2018. A practicing Sikh, he wears a turban to express his faith as he stands in front of portraits of previous mayors in New Jersey's City Hall. *Ismail Ferdous, 2018*

MARYLAND Assateague Island National Seashore is home to more than 300 wild ponies between the Maryland and Virginia sides of the island. Some believe the horses arrived on the island after a Spanish galleon ship sank offshore. *Hannele Lahti, 2006*

LONNIE BUNCH III

When I first came to Washington as a 17-year-old freshman at Howard University, D.C. was unsettling and scary. I had never lived in a city, especially one still on edge from the urban conflagrations of 1968 and disheveled by the massive construction that would soon lead to the Metro. Yet I quickly discovered that D.C. was a city with soul and culture. I reveled in the pace and the poetry of Chocolate City and found joy and inspiration from visiting each of the Smithsonian museums. And when I needed a respite from urban life, there was nothing better than exploring the best city park in America—Rock Creek Park. D.C. is more than the seat of politics; it has become my home.

Lonnie G. Bunch III is the 14th Secretary of the Smithsonian, overseeing 19 museums, 21 libraries, the National Zoo, and numerous research centers. Previously, he served as founding director of the Smithsonian's National Museum of African American History and Culture. Born in Belleville, New Jersey, he has lived in Washington, D.C., since 1970.

WASHINGTON, D.C. Celebrating summer, children jump rope on Fourth Street in Northwest D.C. *Adam Woolfitt, 1983*

OPPOSITE: **CONNECTICUT** Early colonists brought the first pear trees from England to the eastern settlements. Nearly 1.6 billion pounds of the fruit are sold every year in the United States. *Michael Melford, 2008*

PAGE 192: **NEW YORK** Tourists look out from the crown of Lady Liberty—gifted to the United States by France in 1884—to Manhattan's skyline. *William Albert Allard, 1965*

PAGE 193: **PENNSYLVANIA** The torchbearing arm of the Statue of Liberty—sculpted by Frédéric-Auguste Bartholdi—is displayed at the 1876 Centennial Exhibition in Philadelphia. *Centennial Photographic Co., 1876*

191

KAL PENN

New Jersey is about more than the chest-thumping bravado of diverse communities of motivated people. It's also about skiing in the winter. Hiking. Pinning beach badges to bathing suits at the shore, walking barefoot on the board-walk, and working long shifts all summer at a farm on the side of a two-lane road. It's home.

MARYLAND United States Naval Academy graduates throw their caps in the air, a tradition known as the tossing of the "covers," practiced since 1912. After the toss, children race onto the field and claim a hat—graduates often pin inspirational messages to their covers for them. *Annie Griffiths, 2007*

DELAWARE Horseshoe crabs *(Limulus polyphemus)* spawn on the beach of Port Mahon at twilight. *Paul Sutherland, 2010*

NEW JERSEY Prep school students take a rest on the grass during a backpacking expedition through New Jersey's portion of the Appalachian Trail. *Pete Muller, 2016*

BOB IGER

There's nothing like the feeling of being in New York, with its incredible energy, rich history, and the tremendous diversity of cultures, customs, and landscapes. I grew up by the ocean in Long Island and attended college in the bucolic Finger Lakes region, and I spent much of my career amid the swirl and bustle of New York City. From a young age, these experiences—and, more than anything, the wonderful people of New York—have fueled my curiosity, passion, and spirit, as well as my love for the arts, sports, and great food. While I no longer live in New York full-time, I'm proud to say I will always consider it home.

Bob Iger is the executive chairman of the Walt Disney Company; he served as chairman and CEO from 2005 to 2020. He is recognized for growing the company and expanding its global reach with the acquisitions of Pixar, Marvel, Lucasfilm, and 21st Century Fox; the landmark opening of Shanghai Disney Resort in China; and the creation of Disney's direct-to-consumer strategy and successful launch of Disney+. Author of The Ride of a Lifetime, *he was born and raised in Oceanside, New York, and graduated from Ithaca College.*

NEW YORK The iconic 1,250-foot-tall (381 m) Empire State Building has stood above midtown Manhattan since 1931. It took one year and 45 days to build the tower, with workers constructing a framework of four and a half stories per week. *Joe McNally, 2010*

NEW JERSEY Beachgoers spread out across the sand in Ocean City to enjoy the sun and Atlantic Ocean waves. *Amy Toensing, 2003*

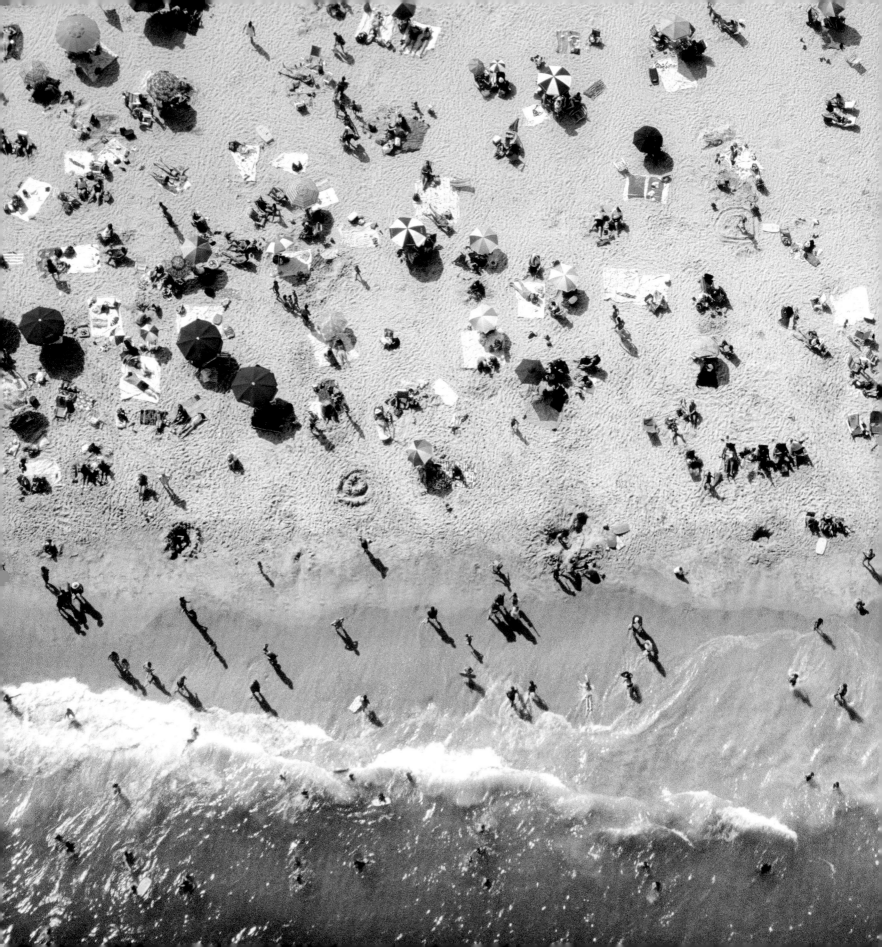

CONNECTICUT The mast of the *Charles W. Morgan*—once part of a 2,700-vessel fleet and now the last wooden whale-ship in the world—rises above the Mystic Seaport. *Brian Drouin, 2006*

MASSACHUSETTS Frost-coated oak leaves and pine needles gather at the edge of Concord's Walden Pond, designated a historic landmark due to its association with Henry David Thoreau's acclaimed book *Walden*.
Tim Laman, 2007

GERALDINE BROOKS

On a night that is supposed to be spring but surely won't feel like it, I will sit down on the hard benches of the West Tisbury elementary school auditorium and decide with my fellow town residents how to run our piece of Martha's Vineyard in the coming year. We'll discuss and vote on issues small and large: Ban the use of single-use plastic bottles? Let dogs share the beach? Increase the school budget? Buy the "herring warden" a new pair of waders? This direct democracy—the give-and-take of discussion with my fellow citizens—is one reason I love living in Massachusetts.

Australian-American journalist and novelist Geraldine Brooks won the 2006 Pulitzer Prize in Fiction for her novel March. *Her other novels,* The Secret Chord, Caleb's Crossing, People of the Book, *and* Year of Wonders *have been critically acclaimed best sellers. She lives by an old mill pond with her two sons, a dog named Bear, and her mare, Valentine.*

MASSACHUSETTS Oak Bluffs police chief Joseph Carter keeps regular tabs on town elder Isabel Powell, a self-proclaimed maker of "wonderful lobster rolls and gorgeous Bloody Marys." *Cary Wolinsky, 2003*

WASHINGTON, D.C. A statue marks a staircase in the Great Hall of the Thomas Jefferson Building, the oldest of the four U.S. Library of Congress buildings, erected between 1890 and 1897. *Robert Bartow, 2013*

VIRGINIA Actors don 18th-century-style dresses as they re-create daily life in Colonial Williamsburg. *Richard Nowitz, 2008*

RHODE ISLAND Just off the shores of Rhode Island, a blue shark *(Prionace glauca)* swims through Atlantic waters. *Brian Skerry, 2012*

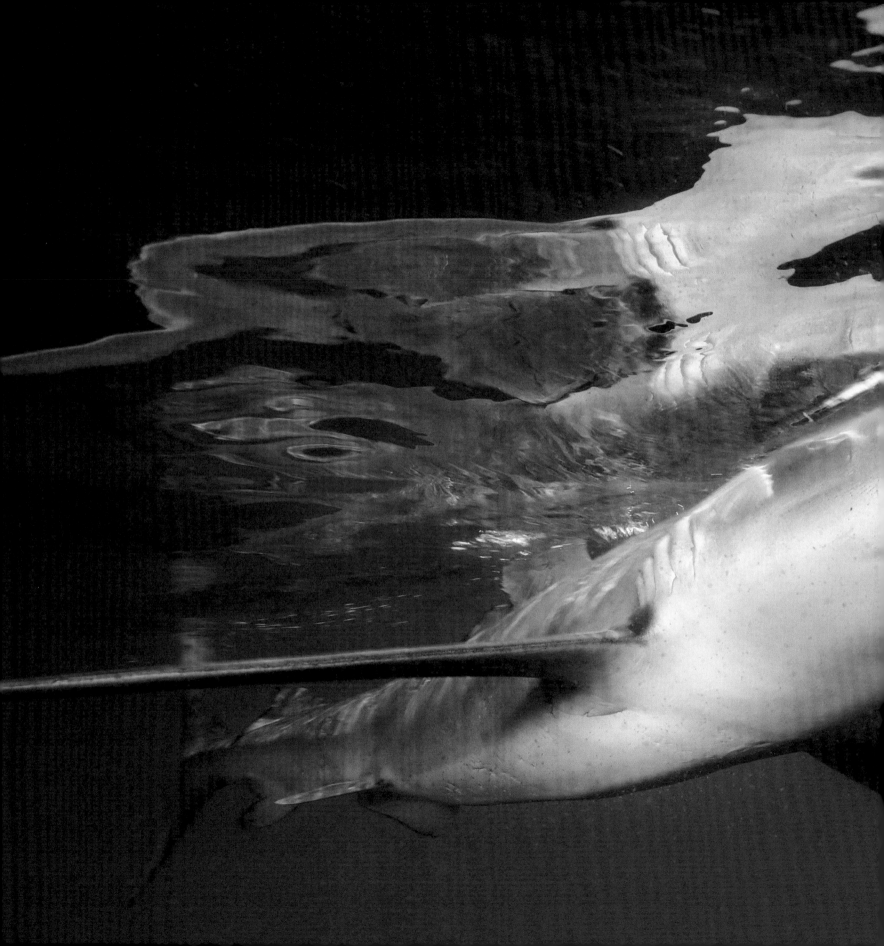

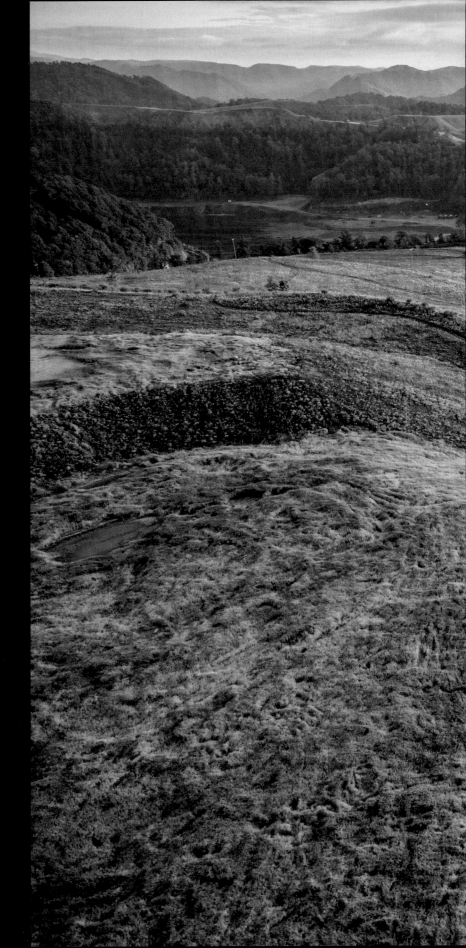

NICK SABAN

I grew up in the small coal-mining town of Monongah, West Virginia, where Booths Creek flows into the West Fork River. There my father taught me the importance of hard work and attention to detail, and those values have paid untold dividends throughout my life. Even though I have been gone for many years, my West Virginia roots helped define my life in more ways than I can count. I met my wife there and learned what it meant to be part of a team.

Nick Saban has been the head football coach at the University of Alabama since 2007. With more than 245 wins under his belt, including five national championships, he is considered one of the greatest and winningest coaches in college football's history. He was raised in Monongah, West Virginia.

WEST VIRGINIA A reclaimed mountain mining summit is planted with non-native grasses. *Robb Kendrick, 2013*

DELAWARE The Old Swedes Church, built in 1699 by Swedish settlers after arriving at Fort Christina—now Wilmington—stands tall above its historic burial grounds. *Michael Melford, 2012*

167

MAINE Atlantic puffins gather together at dawn on the rocks of Eastern Egg Rock Island, where they come to nest. *Melissa Groo, 2018*

VERMONT Hurtling over a snowdrift in Colchester, a snowmobiler flies at a top speed of 45 miles (72 km) an hour. *Emory Kristof, 1967*

ABHI SINHA

Pennsylvania embodies so much American history and culture: It's the birthplace of our Constitution, the home of Valley Forge and Gettysburg, Heinz and the Hershey Company. There's Lake Erie, the Delaware River, the Appalachian Mountains, and some of the most beautiful foliage in America.

For me, Pennsylvania is where I developed my love for sports and the colors Black and Gold, where I made my first lifelong friendships, owned my first dog, and played amateur youth hockey. I will always consider it home.

That my favorite actor, Jeff Goldblum, happens to be from Pittsburgh, like me—well, that's the icing on the cake!

Born in Mumbai, India, Abhi Sinha was raised in Pittsburgh, Pennsylvania, and remains an avid Steelers and Penguins fan. An actor best known for his roles as Vikram in The Social Network, Harry Whitmark *in* The Conjuring 2, *and Ravi Shapur in* The Young and the Restless, *he has also played competitive ice hockey and is a saxophone player.*

PENNSYLVANIA The sun rises in the early morning above downtown Pittsburgh, once a traditional steel industry area. *Lynn Johnson, 1982*

OPPOSITE: MARYLAND Jet trails mark the sky above Baltimore's Inner Harbor, an active port for nearly 200 years and home to the National Aquarium and the Historic Ships in Baltimore's floating maritime history museum. *Deb Felmey, 2012*

PAGE 158: WEST VIRGINIA The Elakala Falls is a series of four cascades of Shay's Run in Blackwater Falls State Park. *Michael Melford, 2017*

PAGE 159: NEW HAMPSHIRE A long exposure captures star trails, with Polaris at the center, above a rock-strewn river. *Babak Tafreshi, 2012*

JOHNNY WEIR

Delaware is a tiny treasure. When I was 12, I moved to Newark, a quaint college town full of youthful energy and life. Year-round I was on the ice, skating at an elite facility with some of the best in the world. In the summer, I could head to the boardwalk to eat fries with malt vinegar or chew on salt water taffy. Today, my home is away from the city, surrounded by rolling hills and pastures. At night, I can hear the sound of the wind, birdsong, hooting owls, or foxes calling to each other. Like many in Delaware, I find comfort in family; I put family first. Delaware can be a rough place too, where you have to work hard to be someone, to make your mark. Living here helps me understand that we have to push ourselves to the limit to make our way in this world, and to appreciate the journey.

Johnny Weir is a two-time Olympic figure skater and three-time U.S. National Figure Skating Champion. He is NBC's lead figure skating commentator and an ambassador to the Olympic Games. A fashion designer and LGBTQ activist, he was raised in Pennsylvania before moving to Delaware. Along with many other film and television appearances, he was the focus of Pop Star on Ice, *a documentary about his career.*

DELAWARE Dolle's has been making its original salt water taffy—as well as fudge, caramel, and brittle—on the Rehoboth Beach boardwalk since 1927. *Stephen St. John, 2011*

NEW JERSEY Jon Bon Jovi and Richie Sambora perform at the 2007 Live Earth concert, a 24-hour event held at Giants Stadium and broadcast live around the globe to raise awareness of climate change. *Jodi Cobb, 2007*

MAINE Two women dressed in boiled-red "shells" and padded "claws" participate in a Lobster Festival pageant at the port of Rockland, which calls itself the "lobster capital of the world." *Luis Marden, 1952*

RHODE ISLAND More than 80 topiaries sculpted in the shapes of animals—including an elephant and llama—adorn the lawn of Newport's Green Animals Topiary Garden on the former estate of Thomas E. Brayton. *Bob Krist, 2003*

ROXANNE QUIMBY

Clinging to the United States by its tenuous border with New Hampshire, Maine is more a part of the wild Atlantic and the Canadian Maritimes than America. A refuge from civilization to the south, it is a safe harbor for the individual spirit to thrive. Thank you, Maine, for not being on the way to anywhere in particular. Just Maine.

Roxanne Quimby moved in 1975 to Maine, where she developed a life-long commitment to a relationship with the great outdoors. She started Burt's Bees in her kitchen, using natural, earth-based ingredients and sustainable packaging.

MAINE Portland Head Light is Maine's oldest lighthouse. It was first lit on January 10, 1791, using 10 whale oil lamps. *Luis Zavala, 2010*

OPPOSITE: VERMONT The 82-foot (25 m), plank-lattice Worrall Covered Bridge, built in 1868, spans the Williams River in Rockingham. *Guy Heitmann, 2015*

PAGE 146: NEW YORK The 71st floor (illuminated here) of the Chrysler Building, completed in 1930, was an observation deck until 1945. It is the uppermost occupied floor of the building, now used by a data and software company. *Nathan Benn, 1988*

PAGE 147: VIRGINIA The Luray Caverns were shaped some 400 million years ago. First discovered by local residents in 1878, they are the largest caverns in the eastern United States. *Kent Kobersteen, 2014*

KATIE COURIC

I had an idyllic "Leave It to Beaver" upbringing in Arlington, Virginia. But the state has come a long way since the Cleavers (and even since I graduated from the University of Virginia in 1979). A hundred years ago, 90 percent of Virginians were born in state; today, a majority were born elsewhere, making it a more vibrant and forward-thinking place. Sometimes tradition makes it difficult to see things in a new light. But this is not your grandfather's Old Dominion. Today, Virginia isn't just for lovers. It's for everyone.

Katie Couric is an award-winning journalist and producer. She was co-anchor of the Today Show on NBC for 15 years before going to CBS and becoming the first woman anchor of a nightly broadcast. She grew up in Arlington, Virginia.

VIRGINIA A junior prince holds his girlfriend's hand as he rides in the back of a car during homecoming festivities at J. E. B. Stuart High School. *Karen Kasmauski, 2001*

VERMONT The Northeast Kingdom of Vermont has been called "a retreat for the eccentric." One of its museums, the Museum of Everyday Life, specializes in everyday objects. *Stéphane Lavoué, 2018*

NEW HAMPSHIRE A building in the town of Sandwich was painted in stars and stripes to celebrate the United States' bicentennial. *Greg Dale, 2015*

WASHINGTON, D.C. On August 28, 1963, Martin Luther King, Jr., stands with other civil rights leaders and his "I Have a Dream" speech in hand during the March on Washington. *James P. Blair, 1963*

CONNECTICUT The blue onion dome of the Colt Armory, a historic firearms factory, towers above the busy Hartford traffic making its way along Interstate 91. *Brian Drouin, 2015*

MARTA KUZMA

When I arrived at the Yale School of Art from Sweden, I was worried that I'd miss the great sprawls of woody Scandinavian wilderness. But when I ventured into Guilford on Connecticut's shoreline, struck by the vastness of the salt marshes inhabited by meadows of ashen blond phragmites that served to filter the mainland from the sea, I was drawn to the area as home. I learned about a birdlife I had not previously known: the snowy egrets that gathered at dusk as a community amid the branches of a sheltered bay along Leetes Island; the occasional red-winged blackbird; the American widgeon; and the nesting osprey within magnificent bundles of sticks, barks, grasses, and algae balanced precariously high on old telephone poles along the coast.

Marta Kuzma was appointed the Stavros Niarchos Foundation Dean and Professor of Art at the Yale School of Art in 2016, the first woman to serve in the position since the school was founded in 1869. She is a curator, artist, and educator. Before coming to Yale she was the vice chancellor and rector of the Royal Institute of Art in Stockholm and director of the Office for Contemporary Art Norway.

CONNECTICUT A great egret stands among colorful grasses on Mason's Island in the fall. *Michael Melford, 2013*

NEW YORK The *Mayflower II*, a reproduction of the 17th-century *Mayflower* ship, enters New York Harbor after a solitary voyage across the Atlantic. Upon arrival, the captain and crew received a ticker tape parade in New York City. *B. Anthony Stewart, 1957*

LAND OF ORIGINS

CONNECTICUT I DELAWARE I MAINE I MARYLAND I MASSACHUSETTS I NEW HAMPSHIRE I NEW JERSEY I NEW YORK I PENNSYLVANIA I RHODE ISLAND I VERMONT I VIRGINIA I WASHINGTON, D.C. I WEST VIRGINIA

Our national journey began in the East, as did Katharine Bates's. Many a scene and many a moment carry us back to those beginnings. Some with archival precision: a reproduction of the *Mayflower,* approaching a coastline now cityscape but once wilderness to be tamed; Wilmington's Old Swedes Church, calling in the faithful since the 1600s; the Library of Congress, its ornate architecture granting elegant solemnity to readers since 1800; the graceful and complicated rigging of the *Charles W. Morgan,* launched in 1841, the last ship ever to go whaling; that gleeful moment, hats tossed in the air, as Navy cadets graduate in Annapolis, an annual ritual going back nearly 200 years.

Floats parade through American streets every Thanksgiving, flags are flown high every Fourth of July, shaping lifetime memories, person by person, likely more grand year after year, but no less meaningful than the shared national past they recall. Subtler reminders of history abound here, too: in special events—proms and parades, county fairs and carnivals—and in the everyday scenes that surround us—old-time-variety fruit hanging from the bough, horses grazing pastoral farmyards, or vintage covered bridges, sturdied up for modern traffic.

Even the natural world speaks of a pride-worthy past. These seem to be the same frostbitten autumn leaves, the same small mist rising muffled over the same shimmering water that welcomed Thoreau during his year in the woods. Puffins still squawk from their rocky cradles, horseshoe crabs still spawn at water's edge, foxes still tiptoe through the underbrush. Life in the East and mid-Atlantic does not linger in the past, though. Witness the Pittsburgh skyline, the kaleidoscope of culture that is New York's Times Square, the spontaneous moments of jump-rope—life happening on every street corner. Day by day, we keep creating a new American history.

OPPOSITE: **PENNSYLVANIA** A group of Amish children pose for an informal portrait on the front steps of their home in Lancaster County. *J. Baylor Roberts, 1937*

PAGES 128-129: **DELAWARE** Mist lingers above the vibrant green trees lining the Brandywine River. *Michael Melford, 2012*

ID-ATLANTIC

O BEAUTIFUL FOR PILGRIM FEET

WHOSE STERN, IMPASSIONED STRESS,

A THOROUGHFARE FOR FREEDOM BEAT

ACROSS THE WILDERNESS!

CHAPTER TWO

THE EAST & M

COLORADO A bald eagle *(Haliaeetus leucocephalus)* soars across a snowy landscape in Basalt. *Robbie George, 2005*

TONY FINAU

Even though I was born and raised in Utah, American Samoa feels like home. It's the history of my family. American Samoa is a beautiful, tropical paradise. There are the islands, the village beside the rock where my mom grew up, and the beaches everywhere. Here, kids play in the sand every day—games of cricket, rugby, volleyball, and football. For Tongan and Samoan people, respect is a big deal, and it is especially shown toward guests. Everyone is your aunt or uncle. Even if you are not related, you treat each other like family. You cannot forget where you come from and I'm humbled to have family roots in Samoa.

Tony Finau, one of seven siblings and a father of four, is the first professional golfer of Samoan and Tongan descent. His family-focused foundation, the Tony Finau Foundation, aims to empower youth through golf and educational resources. On the PGA Tour since 2015, Finau captured his first victory at the 2016 Puerto Rico Open, where he won in a thrilling playoff. He was born in Salt Lake City, Utah, and his first sport was fire-knife dancing, a Samoan ritual.

AMERICAN SAMOA Searching for dinner, a snorkeler hunts clams and sea urchins off the coast of Ofu Island, whose reef sits within the 13,500-acre (5,463.3 ha) National Park of American Samoa. *Randy Olson, 2000*

OPPOSITE: NORTHERN MARIANA ISLANDS Spectators watch a Christmas Eve fireworks display poolside in Saipan. *Mike Ronesia, 2012*

PAGE 120: CALIFORNIA Marijuana growers Nicholas and Richard Lopez tend a small garden plot and take photos of their harvest to share online. *Lynn Johnson, 2015*

PAGE 121: WYOMING A sow and her cub forage for pocket gophers at Fishing Bridge during a snowfall in Yellowstone National Park. *Gary Melnysyn, 2011*

PHIL KNIGHT

The best teacher I ever had, one of the finest men I ever knew, spoke of the Oregon Trail often. "It's our birthright," he'd growl—our DNA. "The cowards never started," he'd tell me, "and the weak died along the way—that leaves us."

Phil Knight founded Nike with his former University of Oregon track coach, Bill Bowerman. He served as chairman and CEO of the company for 52 years and is the current chairman emeritus. He was born and raised in Portland.

OREGON The grandsons of Samuel and Betsy Brown, who made the journey on the Oregon Trail and acquired what would become Gervais, Oregon, stand on the porch of their family's estate with portraits of the pioneers and heirlooms from the trek. *James L. Amos, 1986*

ARIZONA A hiker takes in the view of the Colorado River winding its way through the Grand Canyon at sunset. *Pete McBride, 2016*

AMERICAN SAMOA Young women, dressed in their Sunday best, attend church services at Sailele Congregational Parish. *Randy Olson, 2007*

VAL PANTEAH, SR.

I truly enjoy living in New Mexico with its diversity of people and cultures. As governor of the largest pueblo in New Mexico, I am proud of my people and our unique way of life, where we still practice our Zuni culture and speak our native language. We are indigenous and proud New Mexicans!

Val R. Panteah, Sr. is the governor of the Pueblo of Zuni, which is nestled in a scenic valley about 150 miles (241 km) west of Albuquerque, New Mexico. Previously, he served as a judge for the tribal council in the Pueblo of Zuni.

NEW MEXICO Ladders provide access to the rooftops of households in the Pueblo of Zuni. *Nicholas H. Darton, 1916*

MONTANA Riders walk their horses by a lake, backed by a sunlit mountain range. *Keith Ladzinski, 2015*

WASHINGTON Patos Island is part of the 1,000-acre (405 ha) San Juan Islands National Monument, created by President Obama in 2013. *Michael Melford, 2014*

AMERICAN SAMOA A young boy spreads pandanus palm fronds out to dry; when ready, they will be woven into mats used for sleeping and sitting and often given as gifts. *Randy Olson, 2000*

HILLARY ROBISON

In Wyoming's plains, mountains, and meadows, I've experienced its diverse flora and fauna—from tiny alpine flowers and bustling insects to the majestic bison and grizzly bears. I've watched cutthroat shimmer in streams and seen birds of prey pursue them. I've marveled at its hydrothermal features and paused to honor the history and people of this land. To me, Wyoming is a vast tapestry of natural and cultural wonders that inspire the soul and bring an intense feeling of being free and alive in a world of possibility and hope.

Hillary Robison is the deputy chief of the Yellowstone Center for Resources at Yellowstone National Park. She earned her Ph.D. studying grizzly bear conservation issues in the Greater Yellowstone Ecosystem and previously served as the chief of resources at Western Arctic National Parklands.

WYOMING In the National Elk Refuge near Jackson, Wyoming, an estimated 11,000 elk share their winter ranges with a growing population of bison. *Charlie Hamilton James, 2016*

ARIZONA Prehistoric petroglyphs are carved into rock surfaces along Lithodendron Wash in the Painted Desert of Petrified Forest National Park. *Scott S. Warren, 2014*

CALIFORNIA Artist Salvador Cortez stands in front of his graffiti rendering of Yoda on Solano Alley in Oakland. *Deanne Fitzmaurice, 2014*

IDAHO A young boy, Phillip Goodell, hides behind a hay bale at his father's ranch in Salmon. *Joel Sartore, 1992*

COLORADO A skier carves new tracks into fresh powder in Aspen ski resort's Maroon Bowl. *Pete McBride, 2006*

HAWAII Lava spills from 60 feet (18 m) above into the ocean, creating an explosion from the heat and pressure of the super-heated water. *Patrick Kelley, 2017*

MITT ROMNEY

My life is shaped by the values of my ancestors who sacrificed to settle the great state of Utah, values that remain ingrained in the character of Utahns to this day. The people, paired with the beauty of its majestic landscapes—red-rock canyons, alpine meadows, sprawling salt flats, and towering mountain peaks—make our state an extraordinary place to live, and I am proud to call it home.

Mitt Romney was the Republican nominee for president of the United States in 2012. He is a U.S. senator representing Utah and was governor of Massachusetts from 2003 to 2007. Prior to his time as governor, he led the 2002 Salt Lake Organizing Committee for the Winter Olympics. Raised in Michigan, Romney received his degree at Brigham Young University and has lived in Utah permanently since 2013.

UTAH Vistas of red-rock hoodoos are seen along the Queens Garden Trail in Bryce Canyon National Park. *Richard Maschmeyer, 2016*

OPPOSITE: **OREGON** The Moon Locking Pavilion in Portland's Lan Su Chinese Garden is part of the city oasis's tranquil beauty and the community's appreciation of richly authentic Chinese culture. *Diane Cook and Len Jenshel, 2011*

PAGE 94: **NEW MEXICO** A buffalo herd manager displays his hunting trophies at his home in Santa Fe. *Catherine Karnow, 2004*

PAGE 95: **OREGON** Mary Farnham, an 83-year-old artist suffering from memory loss, continues to paint and draw, including painting the walls of her room in a residential care facility green. *Maggie Steber, 2007*

ROBERT F. SMITH

Growing up as a fourth-generation Coloradan, I learned early on to appreciate the diversity of the state's geography and its people. The ever-present majestic Rocky Mountains, crystal clear rivers and lakes teeming with shimmering rainbow trout and colorful greenback cutthroat trout, dense aspen groves that stretch as far as the eye can see, high plains of sagebrush, stunning canyon lands and plateaus, massive sand dunes and sweeping plains of waving grasses—all made for a backdrop of wonder. People come to Colorado to experience its natural beauty, but they stay for the beauty of its welcoming people who possess a uniquely pioneering spirit.

OPPOSITE: **WYOMING** More than a third of Yellowstone National Park, including the Grand Prismatic Spring, sits within the caldera of an ancient yet still active volcano. *Michael Nichols, 2016*

PAGE 88: **ALASKA** In 1916, the National Geographic Society photographed members of an Alaskan Eskimo group, showcasing their traditional fur attire. *Carl L. Lomen, 1916*

PAGE 89: **NEVADA** Ashley Riggs, photographed in a tintype portrait at 16, grew up and was homeschooled on the 200,000-acre (81,000 ha) Maggie Creek Ranch, where her father is the ranch manager. *Robb Kendrick, 2004*

MARY LAMBERT

I've toured all over the world, but no place has bewitched me like Washington State. There's something in the air—clean and crisp and alive. What a gift to marvel at the majestic Mount Rainier while on a ferry traveling to the peninsula to make music with my friends. I have always wondered: *How on Earth can a place be so beautiful?* And in the summer? It's extraordinary. Come June, it feels like everyone on the street is smiling at each other, like we're all family. The beginning of the thaw. This place, this community, these royal mountains made me the writer I am, and I will always find my way home to the magic of the great Pacific Northwest.

Mary Lambert is a singer, songwriter, and composer who broke out with her Grammy-winning song "Same Love." She is an advocate for both the LGBTQ and mental health communities, and reflects her own candid experiences in her art. Her poetry collection, Shame Is an Ocean I Swim Across, *was released in 2018, and her self-produced album* Grief Creature *was released in 2019. She was raised in Everett, Washington.*

WASHINGTON Snowcapped Mount Rainier stands tall above green meadows of wildflowers. *Colin Brynn, 2017*

NORTHERN MARIANA ISLANDS A squadron of spotted eagle rays swim through the tidal currents in Eagle Ray City off the coast of Tanapag. *David Doubilet, 2014*

NEW MEXICO Snow geese take flight over their wintering grounds within the Bosque del Apache National Wildlife Refuge. *Yva Momatiuk and John Eastcott, 2003*

NEW MEXICO The National Geographic Society sent Willis T. Lee to explore and map New Mexico's Carlsbad Caverns in 1924. His work and photographs brought so much national attention and tourism to the caverns that Congress decreed it a national park in 1930. *Willis T. Lee, 1924*

KILILI SABLAN

Imagine feeling that the land beneath your feet has been home to your ancestors for thousands of years. That is how the people of the Marianas feel every day. As minute as our islands may be in the vastness of the Pacific, they are enduring. And we feel enduringly rooted to them.

Gregorio Kilili Camacho Sablan became the first delegate to the U.S. House of Representatives from the Commonwealth of the Northern Mariana Islands in 2009 and the first Chamorro member of Congress. He was born on the island of Saipan.

NORTHERN MARIANA ISLANDS With a full moon shining above, water cascades from rocky tidal pools at Puntan Laggua, or Parrotfish Point. *Mark D. Robertson, 2012*

OPPOSITE: **NEVADA** Working cowboys take a rest at a chuckwagon on Il Ranch, one of the last of the big ranches in the West. *William Albert Allard, 1982*

PAGE 78: **IDAHO** Firefighter Forrest Behm, a sawyer running a hand crew out of Garden Valley, stands with his saw at a fire camp at Lucky Peak. *Mark Thiessen, 1998*

PAGE 79: **MONTANA** A classic car, custom-painted with red and orange flames, is parked along the roadside in Bearcreek. *David Guttenfelder, 2014*

JEWEL

Alaska is the last frontier. It's a wild, vast land no fence can tame. Alps challenge the sky on the white wings of glaciers, the tips of which touch the taciturn sea in their slow migration. Bent grass tells of a bear's quiet wandering. The songs of wolves fill the night skies. The northern lights are a spectacle beyond any psychedelic. Alaska is one of the last truly wild places, a treasure. A teacher of scale and proportion. Here you remember you are not bigger than nature. You do not control nature. Here you learn the exhale of receding tides and autumn days. The exuberant inhale of salmon rushing rivers. You learn to respect and care for Mother, and in turn you learn what it is to be cared for.

Alaska raised me. Taught me what water weighs as I scrambled from streams with a five-gallon bucket for the garden. Alaska taught me how hard it is to grow food, and how valuable it is. I learned that resilience is diversity, and the dangers of a monoculture. Biodiversity translated into diversity of thought—of adapting by being in tune with the needs of our surroundings. Alaska reminds us what it is to be wild. Nature is never neurotic, it never worries or has anxiety. If I am anxious, I know I am out of harmony with nature. Alaska is always here, reminding us how to be human.

Jewel is an award-winning singer-songwriter, producer, author, and poet. She went from growing up on a homestead in Alaska with no running water to being homeless in San Diego, California, singing in coffee shops to selling more than 30 million albums worldwide.

ALASKA The moon and the aurora borealis shine over a snow-covered Richardson Highway just south of Alaska's Delta Junction. *Steven Miley, 2017*

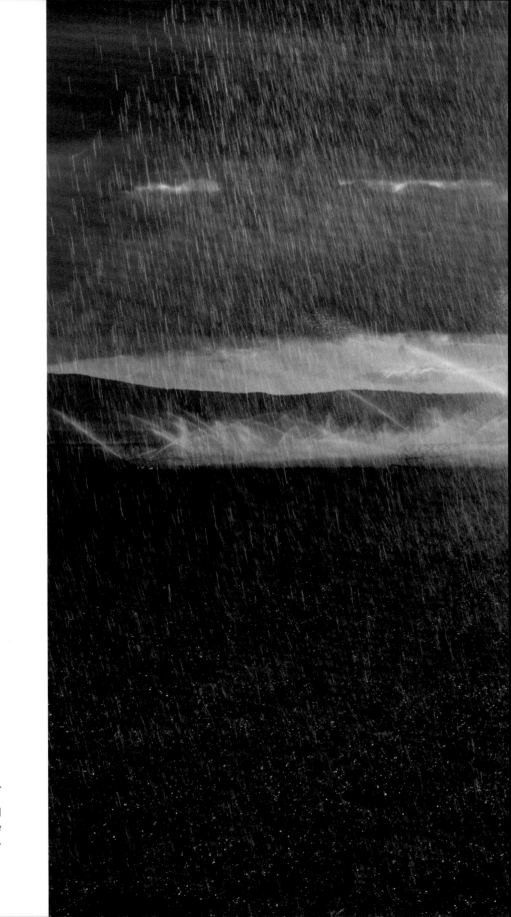

OREGON A quarter-mile-long (0.4 km) irrigation wheel line spritzes an alfalfa field in the Klamath Basin, where more modern techniques are being implemented to nourish fields. *David McLain, 2007*

UTAH Morning light illuminates the ancient desert landscape and red-rock mesas of Canyonlands National Park. *Frans Lanting, 2012*

CALIFORNIA The city of San Francisco glitters beneath a sunset sky as traffic makes its way across the Golden Gate Bridge. *Jonathan Blair, 1966*

CALIFORNIA Scientists snowshoed through Sequoia National Park to measure the President—a 3,200-year-old tree that's 247 feet (75 m) tall and measures 27 feet (8 m) in diameter at its base. *Michael Nichols, 2012*

EDWARD BAZA CALVO

Experience a typical 30-foot (9 m) table of food that you encounter on a visit to village fiestas island-wide and you'll understand what makes Guam so special. The culinary selections include indigenous Chamorro cuisine, together with dishes that originated from places as diverse as the Philippines, Mexico, Japan, Korea, Vietnam, China, America, and Spain.

Like other locals who consider themselves Chamorro, I find the reality is that included with my Chamorro DNA is also the blood of my other ancestors of Spanish, Filipino, Scotch-Irish American, and English descent.

Guam's food reflects its people. Rich with diversity. We are a microcosm of America.

And since we're on the other side of the international date line, Guam truly is "where America's day begins!"

Edward Baza Calvo was born in Tamuning, Guam, and served as the eighth governor of Guam from 2011 to 2019. He also served as a five-term Republican senator within the legislature of Guam.

GUAM A man holds his child in front of a mural being painted on a building, representing the ocean and the island's coconut trees. *Paul Chesley, 2004*

OPPOSITE: COLORADO Luminarias illuminate the Spruce Tree House cliff dwelling, which was constructed between A.D. 1211 and 1278 by ancestral Puebloans and provided shelter for 60 to 80 people. *Ira Block, 2006*

PAGE 64: COLORADO At 360 pounds (163 kg), U.S. national champion weight lifter Shane Hamman demonstrates his phenomenal vertical leap during a training session. *Joe McNally, 2000*

PAGE 65: CALIFORNIA Gina McVey stands with her grandfather's portrait, the American flag from his casket, and a German rifle he obtained fighting as a member of the Harlem Hellfighters, an all-black infantry in World War I. *Ruddy Roye, 2016*

WYOMING A remote camera captures a cougar walking a game trail above the Buffalo Fork River near Grand Teton National Park. *Charlie Hamilton James, 2016*

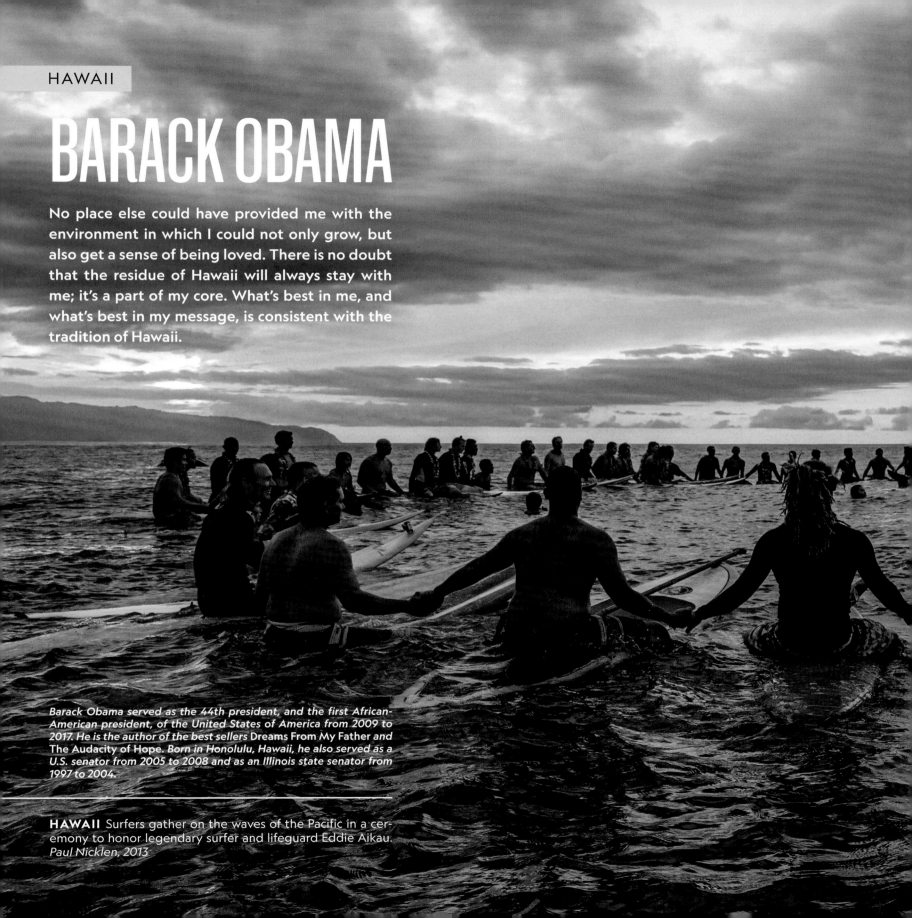

BARACK OBAMA

No place else could have provided me with the environment in which I could not only grow, but also get a sense of being loved. There is no doubt that the residue of Hawaii will always stay with me; it's a part of my core. What's best in me, and what's best in my message, is consistent with the tradition of Hawaii.

Barack Obama served as the 44th president, and the first African-American president, of the United States of America from 2009 to 2017. He is the author of the best sellers Dreams From My Father *and* The Audacity of Hope. *Born in Honolulu, Hawaii, he also served as a U.S. senator from 2005 to 2008 and as an Illinois state senator from 1997 to 2004.*

HAWAII Surfers gather on the waves of the Pacific in a ceremony to honor legendary surfer and lifeguard Eddie Aikau.
Paul Nicklen, 2013

WASHINGTON Sams River Loop Trail in Olympic National Park winds through a forest of vine maple branches coated in lichens and mosses that arch over carpets of wood sorrel. *Melissa Farlow, 2004*

ALASKA A sled dog team races through the Brooks Range in Gates of the Arctic National Park and Preserve, which sits entirely north of the Arctic Circle. *Katie Orlinsky, 2016*

MONTANA A horse's mane blows in the wind as it makes its way through Yellowstone National Park. Horseback riding is among the highest-rated activities in the park. *David Guttenfelder, 2016*

WAYNE NEWTON

Under the brilliant lights of Vegas are the incredible shows, where I've sung and performed thousands and thousands of times. In this "entertainment capital of the world," or the "city of second chances," you can dine on the world's finest cuisine or hope lady luck sidles up beside you at the casino. But Nevada is more than Vegas. It is the Silver State of Dreams. You can ski on water or snow in Tahoe, hike through Red Rock or Great Basin, or make the long climb to the top of the massive Hoover Dam and marvel at our amazing feats and this beautiful country. For all you give us Nevada, *danke schoen!*

Wayne Newton, or "Mr. Las Vegas," is a legendary singer and entertainer. Over the course of 60 years he has performed more than 30,000 shows up and down the Las Vegas Strip on stages in Caesars Palace, the Tropicana, the Stardust, and many others. His song "Danke Schoen" hit number 13 on the Billboard 100 in 1963.

NEVADA The hood of a 1972 Cadillac reflects neon lights of the original Strip as it cruises through Las Vegas. *Michael Nichols, 2001*

ALASKA The Blanket Toss ceremony ends the day at the Nalu-kataq Whaling Festival in Barrow. The festival celebrates the Inupiat whale hunting season and is usually held around the summer solstice. *Patrick Endres, 2016*

GUAM In colorful floral attire, three sisters stand together to watch a local dance festival. *Paul Chesley, 2004*

ARIZONA A Zuni woman dresses in finery, including heirloom turquoise rings and bracelets, for a celebration. *Joseph H. Bailey, 1987*

IDAHO A pack of gray wolves (*Canis lupus*) walk through a meadow in Idaho's Sawtooth Mountains. Once believed to be extinct in Idaho, there are now approximately 1,000 wolves in the state. *Jim and Jamie Dutcher, 2001*

MAYA RUDOLPH

I grew up in sunny Southern California where the avocados grow in backyards and no one seems to own a winter coat. My parents came here in the 1970s to make music and raise their two kids in the quiet canyon just a windy road above the city lights. We spent hot summers in backyard pools, barbecuing and running barefoot through green grass yards that smelled like eucalyptus and grapefruit trees. I sold lemonade on my block and roller-skated through every one of my neighbors' driveways. In the north, I drove up the coast to stand small beside massive coastal redwoods that kept the chilly Pacific Ocean company. People always think I'm a New Yorker, which is funny to me because I'm so much a Californian. I know where to get a good burrito. I've been singing all my life in a car. And I understand the space and quiet. And the light . . . oh the golden light.

Maya Rudolph is an award-winning actress, comedian, and singer. A former member of the band The Rentals, she was a cast member on Saturday Night Live from 2000 to 2007 and has starred in critically acclaimed films including Bridesmaids and Wine Country. She was raised in the Westwood neighborhood of Los Angeles and graduated from the University of California, Santa Cruz.

CALIFORNIA Free-solo climber Alex Honnold stretches on the Ahwahnee Boulders in Yosemite National Park. *Jimmy Chin, 2017*

HAWAII A man displays his tattoos—inked by the traditional Hawaiian method of *kakau,* or hand-tapping—that tell his life story. *Paul Nicklen, 2015*

NEW MEXICO Changing winds form cross-grooves in sand dunes at White Sands National Park, a 275-square-mile (712 sq km) stretch of desert officially registered as a national park in December 2019. *Yva Momatiuk and John Eastcott, 2008*

DAVID QUAMMEN

Montana is wondrous, though not for everybody. In a good year, we have a white Halloween and a white Easter. That can be hard on the non-native maples and elms, if they're in leaf, but the spruces and firs laugh it off. Then again, I'm non-native too. I came in 1973, for the trout fishing, and I've stayed for the snow and the cold and the bracing Scandinavian gloom.

David Quammen is an award-winning author and journalist who has penned more than 15 books, including The Song of the Dodo, Spillover, *and* The Tangled Tree. *He has written for* National Geographic, Outside, Harper's, *and* Rolling Stone, *among others. Born in Cincinnati, Ohio, he calls Montana his home.*

MONTANA A low-lying mist hovers over snow-covered spruces and firs in Montana's portion of Yellowstone National Park. *Robbie George, 2014*

NEVADA A man takes an evening lap in a Las Vegas swimming pool, while others gather to chat. *Pete McBride, 2009*

HAWAII A Filipino pineapple harvester, who came to Maui in 1965, takes a break from the day's work to smoke a cigar. *Gordon Gahan, 1971*

33

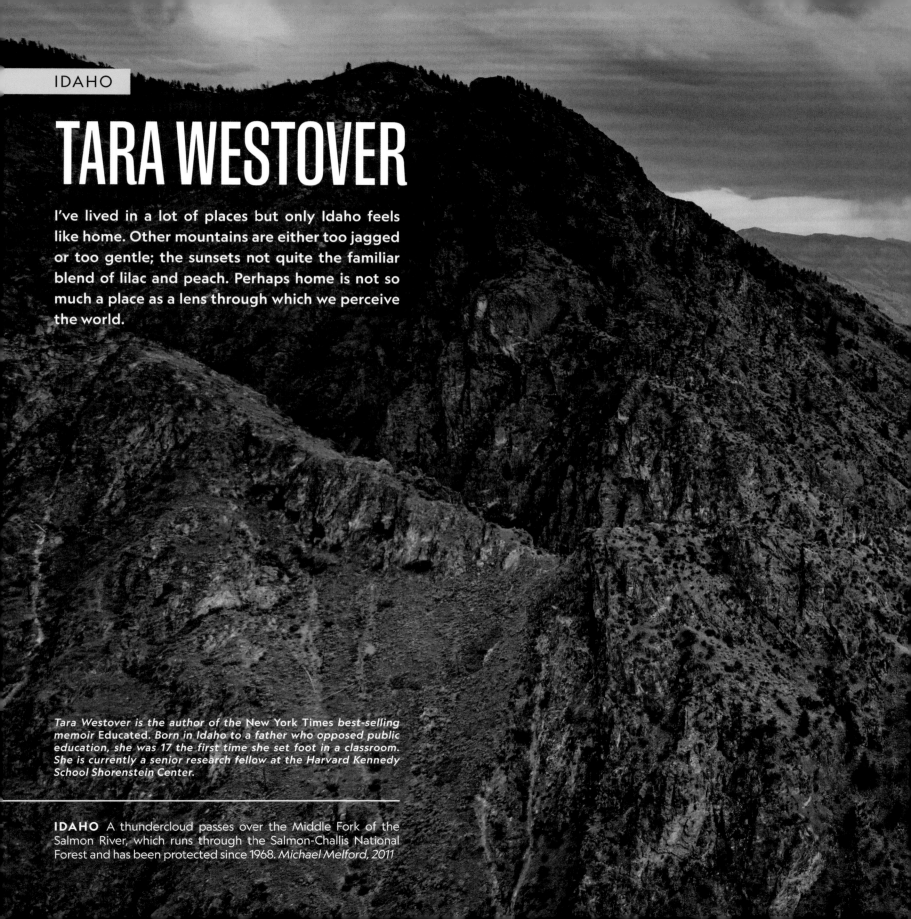

TARA WESTOVER

I've lived in a lot of places but only Idaho feels like home. Other mountains are either too jagged or too gentle; the sunsets not quite the familiar blend of lilac and peach. Perhaps home is not so much a place as a lens through which we perceive the world.

Tara Westover is the author of the New York Times best-selling memoir Educated. Born in Idaho to a father who opposed public education, she was 17 the first time she set foot in a classroom. She is currently a senior research fellow at the Harvard Kennedy School Shorenstein Center.

IDAHO A thundercloud passes over the Middle Fork of the Salmon River, which runs through the Salmon-Challis National Forest and has been protected since 1968. *Michael Melford, 2011*

OREGON A worker harvests pinot noir grapes in Oregon's 150-mile-long (241 km) Willamette Valley, which is home to more than 500 wineries and known for its world-class pinot noir. *Mark Stone, 2018*

ARIZONA With the season's first cut only days away, the pressure is on at an intersquad game at the Milwaukee Brewers' minor-league training facility near Phoenix. *William Albert Allard, 1991*

WASHINGTON Seattle's glass and steel skyscrapers shine in crisp light. *Mark Stone, 2018*

LAND OF PROMISE

ALASKA | AMERICAN SAMOA | ARIZONA | CALIFORNIA | COLORADO | GUAM | HAWAII | IDAHO | MONTANA | NEVADA |
NEW MEXICO | NORTHERN MARIANA ISLANDS | OREGON | UTAH | WASHINGTON | WYOMING

Though vastly more developed and accessible than when Katharine Bates gazed on their purple mountain majesties, these vistas still belong to the wild. Wolves roam Idaho's forest edges. Thousand-year-old sequoias stand tall and grow taller still. Eerie auroras paint the Alaska skies; steam billows from otherworldly hot springs; above all beams the sun in daytime, the cool yellow moon at night. Red-hot lava plunges into turquoise waters.

The American West is a land of distances, surprises, and extremes. Winding canyons, shifting sand dunes, red rock steeples perched precariously. Landscapes of many colors stretch out like endless waves of grain, much farther than the eye can see. Some open wide, plains abundant with fruit and fauna. A glorious blush of spring mountain lilies blooms under the gaze of snow-topped peaks. Look elsewhere and you discover views just as endless but more likely to close in upon us: temperate rainforests where fern-draped trees bend down toward fertile soil; limestone caves where crusty stalactites drip and grow in slow motion. Even the cities of glass and steel, neon, noise, and traffic seem vistas of a sort: pioneer hopes of progress and possibility that throb all day and all night.

Expressions of identity and talent are honored here: Havasupai women chant and dance to age-old rhythms. Samoan girls dressed all in white reflect on Scripture's meaning. An artist's bold graffiti creations grace the city streets of Oakland. Centuries-old traditions are carried on by Alaska's Inupiat, surfers clutching hands to memorialize a life spent on Pacific waves, a woman draped in an American flag to honor her grandfather's heroism in World War I.

To share these vistas and this heritage is to share the promise of America in the long view.

OPPOSITE: **WYOMING** A barn built by settlers John and T. A. Moulton around 1916 sits in the Mormon Row historic district inside Grand Teton National Park. *Robbie George, 2008*

PAGES 22-23: **UTAH** Some conservationists want Lake Powell to be completely drained, allowing plants and wildlife to thrive in the Glen Canyon National Recreation Area. *Michael Melford, 2006*

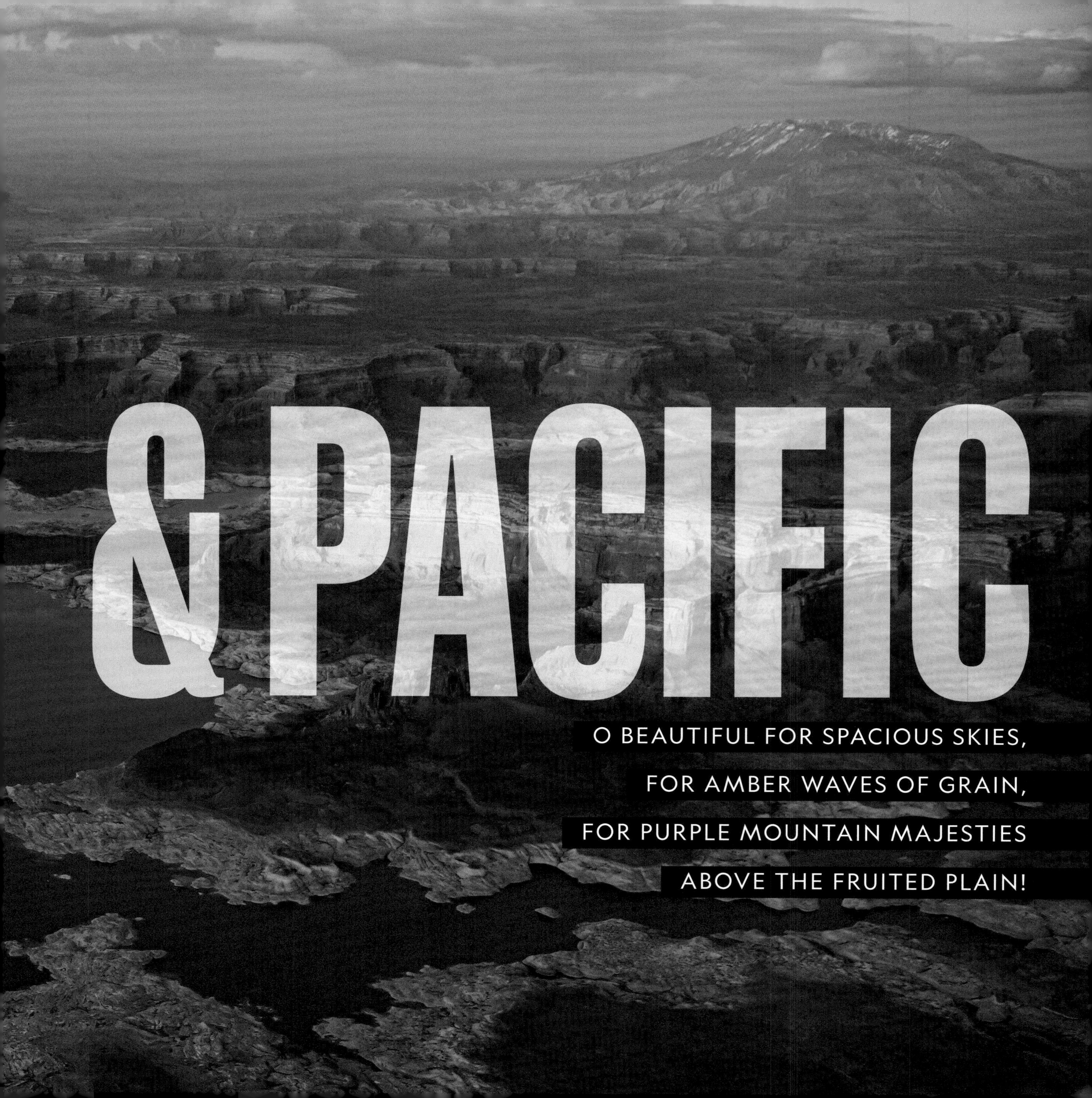

&PACIFIC

O BEAUTIFUL FOR SPACIOUS SKIES,

FOR AMBER WAVES OF GRAIN,

FOR PURPLE MOUNTAIN MAJESTIES

ABOVE THE FRUITED PLAIN!

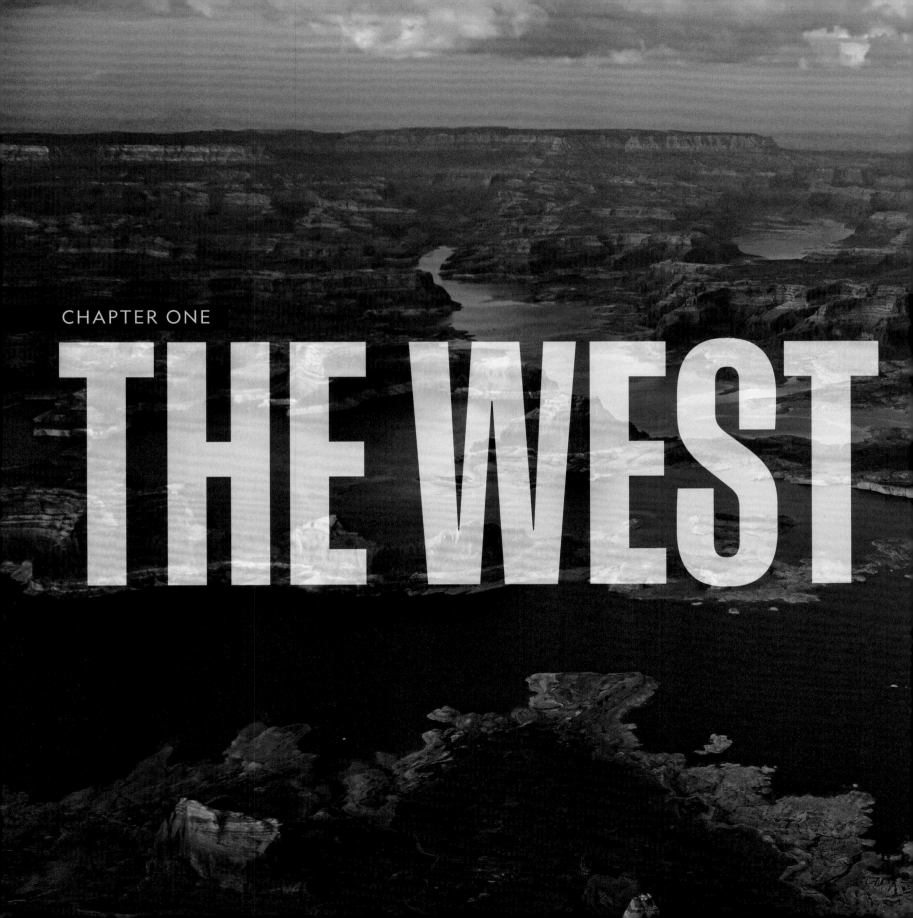

CHAPTER ONE

THE WEST

end.") After Coman's death, Bates wrote, "My own life died, . . . and I seem always to be, as now, listening, alone, from a far-off place, to the glad or excited or passionate voices, yet all the more aware of the beauty and the pathos of humanity." Something they had shared died with Coman, something that had helped Bates find the beauty in the world, and the beauty in America.

Years before, on that summer's day, July 22, 1893, they'd started out at dawn. "Dear Soul who found earth sweet," Bates wrote in *Yellow Clover*, "Remember by love's grace, . . .

How suddenly we halted in our climb,
Lingering, reluctant, up that farthest hill,
Stopped for the blossoms closest to our feet,
And gave them as a token
Each to each,
In lieu of speech.

The higher they climbed, the colder the air, the thinner the trees. The summit was as bare as a glacier, except for a little house, no more than a hut, built of stone, and nearly empty but for a telegraph machine. Bates posted a telegram to her mother. "Greeting from Pikes Peak. Glorious. Dizzy. Wish you were here. Katharine B.C." It seems to have been how the two Katharines signed off together: Katharine Bates and Katharine Coman. Katharine B.C. It's as if "America, the Beautiful," had not one author, but two.

I like, anyway, to picture them there together, huddled against the wind, on top of the world, as if they could see from sea to shining sea, clutching yellow clover. They thought of the country differently. Coman could more easily see its errors, its violence, its bitter divisions; Bates could more easily appreciate its nobility, its ingenuity and invention and the greatness of its ideas. But they both loved it, all the same. Bates later added a few new lines, "America! America! / God mend thine ev'ry flaw." Coman would have liked that.

AMERICA, THE BEAUTIFUL
Katharine Lee Bates

O beautiful for spacious skies,
For amber waves of grain,
For purple mountain majesties
Above the fruited plain!
America! America!
God shed His grace on thee,
And crown thy good with brotherhood
From sea to shining sea!

O beautiful for pilgrim feet
Whose stern, impassioned stress,
A thoroughfare for freedom beat
Across the wilderness!
America! America!
God mend thine every flaw,
Confirm thy soul in self-control,
Thy liberty in law!

O beautiful for heroes proved
In liberating strife,
Who more than self their country loved,
And mercy more than life!
America! America!
May God thy gold refine
Till all success be nobleness,
And every grain divine!

O beautiful for patriot dream
That sees beyond the years,
Thine alabaster cities gleam
Undimmed by human tears!
America! America!
God shed His grace on thee,
And crown thy good with brotherhood
From sea to shining sea!

"Cotton Mills Closing." In those years, railroad workers struck, on average, once a year, and some 2,000 railroad men were killed on the job and 20,000 injured. A railroad workers union founded in 1893 would go on to become the Socialist Party of America.

Bates's first draft of "America, the Beautiful," lavishes its love on the stops she made on that trip from Boston to Colorado Springs: the "music-hearted sea" of Niagara; "thine alabaster cities"—the White City that she'd seen in Chicago; the "amber waves of grain" she'd seen in the Kansas prairie; the "purple mountain majesties" of the Rockies. Fundamentally, too, Bates honored American history as a march of freedom, "O beautiful for pilgrim feet / ... A thoroughfare for freedom beat." She celebrated the courage of American pioneers, the steadfastness of the American spirit. "America, the Beautiful," is also, passionately, a religious poem, one that gives thanks and asks for blessing: "God

shed His grace on thee." But Bates's first draft of the poem—each of her drafts of the poem—contains, too, a critique of the United States. She asks that God give His grace on America, "Till selfish gain no longer stain, / The banner of the free!" Bates's beautiful America had sinned, and its sin was greed.

The best poetry Katharine Lee Bates ever wrote appeared in a book called *Yellow Clover*, a book of love poems she wrote in memory of Katharine Coman. Coman had gotten breast cancer. She endured two mastectomies, at a time when the surgery was experimental, and particularly horrible. Bates nursed her until her terrible, agonizing death. ("We let you suffer long before we called / On morphine, life's last mercy, lest / It fail you ere the

COLORADO A long and narrow road leads from Pikes Peak through the desert. *Craft Shop, 1917*

the study of the American West. They lived together for 25 years. From a third-floor study in the house where Bates displayed the souvenirs of her many travels, Coman wrote her best books, including *The Industrial History of the United States*. Coman, born on a farm in Ohio, was the daughter of an abolitionist. She was a formidable intellectual—Bates once wrote that her eyes had "the strength of folded granite"—and she was a political activist. She helped organize the Chicago Garment Workers' Strike, and, with Bates, she set up immigrant aid societies in Boston. Coman was also a socialist.

Coman and Bates didn't always agree about politics: Coman always took the side of labor against capital, but Bates, as her earliest biographer put it, "privately felt that there were two sides to every question and that after all there was something to be said for capitalism." Still, they shared a profound Christian faith, and they were both entirely immersed in the world of Progressive era social and political reform. Then, too, Bates's love of the wilderness, in particular, was influenced by Coman, who taught a course on "the wastes involved in the exploitation of forests, mineral resources, soil and water power, and the means proposed for scientific conservation," helping to found a field that would later be called environmental science.

In July 1893, when Katharine Lee Bates's train got to Chicago, she stopped to meet Coman, who was there visiting her family. Together, they toured the Columbian Exposition, which had been mounted the year before to honor the 400th anniversary of the voyage of Christopher Columbus. Its features, spread over 600 acres (242.8 ha) of fairgrounds, included a White City, immortalized in "America, the Beautiful" as "thine alabaster cities." Not mentioned in Bates's poem are the fair's many other exhibits, which included more than 400 indigenous Americans on display in what amounted to human zoos, exhibits that had elicited protest. Potawatomi Simon Pokagon sold at the fair a booklet he printed on white birch bark, called "The Red Man's Rebuke," in which he bitterly informed "the pale-faced race that has usurped

our lands and homes, that we have no spirit to celebrate with you the great Columbian Fair."

Coman had long been "warmly interested in the progress of colored people." So it's hard to imagine that Bates, touring the grounds with her, didn't notice that, in the era of Jim Crow, the fair was racially segregated: only the janitors were black—the janitors plus the African Americans who appeared in a series of displays devoted to the history of slavery, or those who were posed, nearly naked, in fake African villages. Frederick Douglass was slated to speak at a designated "Colored People's Day." After the Civil War, Douglass had called for a new vision of America, his own America, the beautiful. "I want a home here not only for the negro, the mulatto and the Latin races; but I want the Asiatic to find a home here in the United States, and feel at home here, both for his sake and for ours," he'd said. And yet in 1882 Congress had passed the Chinese Exclusion Act, banning immigration from China, and states had begun passing the first Jim Crow laws, enforcing strict racial segregation, and, notwithstanding the 14th and 15th Amendments, denying black men the right to vote.

In 1893, when Douglass was invited to speak at the Columbian Exposition, he hoped to speak about all of that, but Mississippi-born Ida B. Wells, founder of the newspaper *Free Speech* and best known for her fearless campaign against lynching, tried to persuade Douglass to turn down the invitation. He went ahead anyway. "Men talk of the Negro problem," he began, but "there is no Negro problem. The problem is whether the American people have loyalty enough, honor enough, patriotism enough, to live up to their own Constitution."

Katharine Lee Bates never saw that speech. She'd left for Colorado by then. She'd traveled on from Chicago alone, but a few days after she arrived, Coman joined her; she taught at Colorado College that summer, too. The two women went everywhere together. "We loved it all!" Bates would write in her diary. They read the newspapers together, too, following news of a financial collapse, the Panic of 1893. "Hard Times," read the headlines.

surefooted mules. At last, they reached the summit, a view she took in, she later said, in "one ecstatic gaze": below, a bedspread of green pine; in the distance, peaks capped with white; above, a sky the blue of a robin's egg. She wrote one line more in her diary that day: "Most glorious scenery I ever beheld." That night, in her room at the Antlers Hotel, she began composing a poem.

America, the Beautiful," Bates's poem, set to music, became the United States' unofficial anthem, a hymn of love of country. There are plenty of better poems about America, the land and the people, including Walt Whitman's "For You O Democracy," written on the eve of the Civil War: "I will plant companionship thick as trees along all the rivers of America, / and along the shores of the great lakes, and all over the prairies, / I will make inseparable cities with their arms about each other's necks." You can hear the echoes of Whitman in Bates. You can hear an answer to both of them—an indictment of both of them—in Langston Hughes's 1936 poem "Let America Be America Again": "O, let America be America again— / The land that never has been yet— / And yet must be—the land where *every* man is free." And you can hear a very different confession of love in Shirley Geok-lin Lim's 1998 poem "Learning to Love America": "because my son will bury me here / because countries are in our blood and we bleed them / because it is late and too late to change my mind / because it is time."

Countries are in our blood and we bleed them. Lim's poem sounds, at first, more raw than "America! America! God shed His grace on thee," as if Bates's poem dates to a simpler America. It does not. Americans of Katharine Lee Bates's day were as politically divided as Americans of this day—arguably, they were more divided—over everything from immigration to land use to racial justice to economic inequality. And her America was similar to this America in more ways, too: It was wondrous and cruel, rich and poor, merciless and merciful, beautiful and ugly. Quite what Bates meant, in each line of the poem, is worth pondering, because the poem is a window to another America, and also, in its way, a mirror to our own. In writing about beauty, I like to think Professor Bates took a cue from her beloved *Hamlet* (Act III, Scene 1): "Could beauty, my lord, have better commerce than with honesty?"

Katharine Lee Bates inherited, as every American does, a struggle for justice. She was born on the seaside, in Falmouth, Massachusetts, spitting distance from the ocean, in the summer of 1859, just weeks before a white-haired self-professed messiah named John Brown and a band of black abolitionists raided a U.S. arsenal at Harpers Ferry, Virginia, in an attempt to collect and distribute enough guns to incite a massive slave rebellion in the Southern states. She was the youngest of five children. Her father was a Congregational minister; her mother, who, astonishingly, for the time, had a college degree, had been a schoolteacher.

The Civil War broke out when Katie was still a baby. She hadn't yet turned six when John Wilkes Booth shot Abraham Lincoln. In 1868, when Katie was nine, her mother gave her a little red notebook. The 14th Amendment, ratified that year, guaranteed the equal protection of the law, regardless of race, but made no provision for the equality of the sexes. In the pages of her little red notebook, nine-year-old Katie reflected on the political status of women. "I am happy to say they have become impatient under the restraint men put upon them," she wrote. "The great question of women's rights has arisen."

It might have been that spark that led the Bates family to do something unusual. Katie's father died when she was a baby, and, at a time when boys were far more likely than girls to get an education, Katie's brothers worked so that Katie could go to school. In 1885, at 26, she became a professor. Two years later, she published her first book of poetry.

At Wellesley, Bates fell in love with another young professor, Katharine Ellis Coman, an economic historian who specialized in

FROM SEA TO SHINING SEA

JILL LEPORE

Katharine Lee Bates, a professor of English at Wellesley College, had a chestnut-eyed collie named Hamlet and a green parrot named Polonius. She taught Shakespeare, and she wrote poetry. She loved to travel. At her rambling Victorian house, a brisk walk from campus, she kept dozens of souvenirs, propped up on the mantel, displayed in glass-doored cabinets: a brass Buddha from China, an alabaster urn from an Egyptian tomb, a bottle of sand from Panama. She made a list of her favorites in a little inventory she once typed up, everything from "a lamp bought from a boy in Nazareth" to "a tin slate of a verse from the Koran." On her desk she kept a framed portrait of Dante; she'd picked it up in Florence.

She'd been to Syria. She'd toured Palestine. She'd ridden a camel in Damascus. She'd hiked the Alps. She'd even seen the Dead Sea. But Katharine Lee Bates is best remembered for a single trip she took in 1893, a pilgrimage across the United States, and for the poem she wrote about that trip. She had an eye for grandeur and for wonder, for landscape and miniature, the poet's version of the photographer's eye that's on display on every page of this extraordinary volume from National Geographic's matchless archive, a book that captures the delicate immensity of the Gateway Arch in St. Louis; boys in a schoolroom, dressed as Malcolm X; a woman marching in a parade, wearing a dress made of a sequined Puerto Rican flag; and scientists scaling a redwood in Sequoia National Park, dangling, as if by a thread—each another illustration of the beauty, vulnerability, variety, and dignity of the people and of the land.

She left Boston by train on June 29, 1893. The next day, she felt on her face the mist of one of the world's most stunning wonders and wrote in her diary about "the glory and the music of Niagara Falls." "Reached Chicago," she wrote two days later, from the site of a world's fair, the Columbian Exposition. She spent July 4 in the prairie, in western Kansas, eyeing its amber waves of grain. She wrote in her diary that she considered herself "a better American for such a Fourth." The next day, she reached Colorado Springs, at the foot of the Rocky Mountains, in all their purple majesty.

She'd agreed to lecture on Chaucer for the summer, at Colorado College. She taught her course and then, near the end of July, she went on an expedition to the Garden of the Gods, where red sandstone rises out of the earth in formations that look like so many cathedral spires. She headed next to a 14,115-foot (4,302 m) mountain called Tava, or Sun Mountain, by the Ute. "Pikes Peak or Bust," she wrote in her diary. She boarded a horse-drawn prairie wagon: Halfway up, the driver switched out the horses for more

---

OPPOSITE: **COLORADO** A juniper tree frames the South Gateway Rock in the Garden of the Gods Visitor and Nature Center. *Keith Ladzinski, 2005*

OPPOSITE: WASHINGTON A powwow regalia at White Swan is made of beaded embroidery and federally regulated eagle feathers. *David Alan Harvey, 1994*

PAGE 1: WASHINGTON, D.C. While under repair in 2014, the United States Capitol's dome was covered in scaffolding—except for the Statue of Freedom at its top. *Sam Kittner, 2014*

PAGES 2-3: ALASKA Chikuminuk Lake reflects the raw wilderness of 1.6-million-acre (650,000 ha) Wood-Tikchik State Park, one of the largest state parks in the United States. *Michael Melford, 2010*

HAWAII A pod of spinner dolphins *(Stenella longirostris)* swim through the tropical waters off the coast of Oahu. *Brian Skerry, 2013*

INDIANA Contestants line up for judging in the dairy goat competition at the Indiana State Fair. Indiana was the sixth state to host a fair, which has been held annually in Indianapolis since 1852. *Vincent J. Musi, 2010*

GEORGIA Spanish moss covers an old live oak tree on Cumberland Island, the largest of Georgia's Sea Islands.
Michael Melford, 2004

NEW YORK Lending to the nickname "The City That Never Sleeps," the bright lights of New York City's Times Square illuminate Broadway show billboards and flashy advertisements. *Fraser Hall, 2017*

PUERTO RICO A woman looks out to a double rainbow from the walls of the Castillo San Felipe del Morro, also known as El Morro, in San Juan. *Stephen Alvarez, 2014*

E BEAUTIFUL

A STORY IN PHOTOGRAPHS

NATIONAL GEOGRAPHIC

WASHINGTON, D. C.

AMERICA TH

FOREWORD BY JILL LEPORE